Third Grade
FOUNDATIONS

GRADE **3**

American Education Publishing™
An imprint of Carson-Dellosa Publishing LLC
Greensboro, North Carolina

American Education Publishing™
An imprint of Carson-Dellosa Publishing LLC
P.O. Box 35665
Greensboro, NC 27425 USA

ISBN 978-1-62399-079-4

02-147137784

Table Of Contents

Table Of Contents

Table Of Contents

Table Of Contents

In third grade, your child will begin to take the information he or she has learned so far and put it together into more complicated concepts. Beginning in the third grade, children will become increasingly more abstract thinkers. This school year places a heavy emphasis on past, present, and future as it relates to all subjects.

Third Grade Foundations offers activities for a full year of practice. The practice pages are simple and engaging, providing hours of learning fun. Many activities also connect with science or social studies for a wide range of learning. With *Third Grade Foundations*, your child is getting a well-rounded supplement to his or her education.

Language Arts

By the third grade, your child can read with fluency. Now, he or she will move away from "learning to read" and begin "reading to learn," by taking on chapter books and non-fiction texts. With *Third Grade Foundations*, your child will gain a full year of practice with these important skills.

In third grade, your child will learn:

- to produce simple, compound, and complex sentences. **page 35**
- to explain the function of nouns, pronouns, verbs, adjectives, and adverbs in general and their functions in particular sentences. **pages 38-43**
- to determine the main idea of a text, recount the key details, and explain how they support the main idea. **pages 47-49**
- to ask and answer questions to demonstrate understanding of a text, referring explicitly to the text as the basis for the answers. **pages 70-73**

Use the following hands-on activities to practice language arts skills with your child. These activities encourage creativity and logical thinking. Keep in mind that the process, not the finished product, is what is important!

- When your child finishes a book, create fun ways to share the information in the book with a friend. Some ways to do this might be to write a letter from one character to another, create a comic strip illustrating the events of the book, or write a journal entry one of the characters might write.
- Invite your child to write a different ending or new chapter to a story. If your child can do this in a logical manner, he or she has grasped the plot or ideas presented. write a journal entry one of the characters might write.

Math

In the third grade, your child will be focusing on four key areas: multiplication and division within 100, fractions and decimals, area, and two-dimensional shapes. With *Third Grade Foundations*, your child will practice math skills that are fundamental to learning these concepts.

In third grade, your child will learn:

- to fluently multiply and divide within 100. By the end of third grade, your child should know from memory all products of two one-digit numbers. **pages 115–124**
- to understand a fraction 1/b as the quantity formed by 1 part when a whole is partitioned into *b* equal parts. **pages 141–145**
- to recognize and generate simple equivalent fractions. **page 143**
- to measure and estimate liquid volumes and masses of objects using standard units of grams (g), kilograms (kg), and liters (l). **page 150**
- to partition shapes into parts with equal areas and express the area of each part as a unit fraction of the whole. **page 156**
- to solve real world and mathematical problems involving perimeters of polygons. **page 157**

Your child will become more interested in math if he or she can see how it applies to life outside of school. Here are fun ways to practice age-appropriate math with your child throughout each day:

- Using the sports section of the newspaper, help your child locate times from swim meets, track meets, auto races, and so on. Point out that the times are in tenths and hundredths of seconds. Have your child practice adding and subtracting the times of sporting events.
- Use foods such as pizza, cake, pie, and brownies to help your child identify halves, fourths, thirds, and so on. Practice adding and subtracting like fractions. For example, "If Sally takes $\frac{1}{6}$ of the pie and Jane takes $\frac{2}{6}$ of the pie, how much of the pie is gone? How much of the pie is left over?"

All About Town

Directions: This map shows the stops a bus makes on its route from North Station to South Station. Write the names of the stops in alphabetical order to figure out what route the bus traveled. Then, trace the bus route.

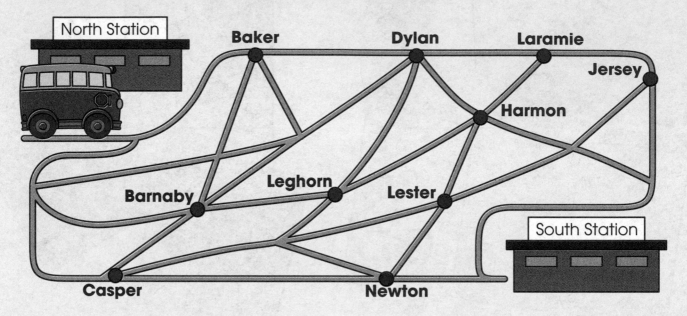

1. _____

2. _____

3. _____

4. _____

5. _____

6. _____

7. _____

8. _____

9. _____

10. _____

Try This!

Look at a map of your state.
On another sheet of paper, write the names of 20 cities in alphabetical order.

Clowning Around

Directions: Add a word part from the word bank to each blend to make a word that describes something a clown might do in his act.

| _ink | _y | _ow |
| _imb | _asp | _ip |

bl   **fl**   **cl**

_____   _____   _____

_____   _____   _____

On another sheet of paper, write a list of action words that start with *bl*, *cl*, or *fl*.

Try This!

Twelve Swans Standing Still

Directions: Write the two letters that make up each word's beginning blend. Write **st**, **sw**, or **tw**.

1. _____

2. _____

3. _____

4. _____

5. _____

6. _____

Try This!

On another sheet of paper, write five sentences that include as many words starting with *st*, *sw*, or *tw* as possible. For example: Twins stood on stools in matching sweaters.

Stay on the Path

Directions: Write **ow** or **ou** to correctly complete each word.

1. sc _____ t

2. m _____ ntain

3. tr _____ t

4. fl _____ er

5. sh _____ t

6. sh _____ er

7. t _____ er

8. c _____ nt

On another sheet of paper, write a story about a hike in the mountains.
Use as many *ou* and *ow* words as possible.

Say Cheese!

Directions: Write **ch**, **sh**, or **th** to complete each word.

_____umb

_____irt

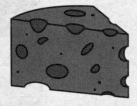

_____eese

_____oe

_____orn

_____eck

_____in

_____ell

_____ermos

Try This!

On another sheet of paper, list five other words for each of the beginning digraphs *ch*, *sh*, and *th*.

Scavenger Hunt

Directions: Part of a scavenger hunt list was torn. Figure out what needs to be found by completing each word with the **ft**, **nt**, or **st** ending.

1. te _____

2. ne _____

3. ra _____

4. a _____

5. pla _____

6. fore _____

7. something so _____

8. footpri _____

On another sheet of paper, write four more words with *ft*, *nt*, or *st* blends. Using those words, write a story about a boy who has gone on a scavenger hunt.

Inch Along

Directions: Circle the word that names each picture.

couch   pouch   bush   brush   mouse   mouth

wreath   wrist   bath   bash   ditch   dish

beach   bench   fish   wish   clock   cloth

Try This!

Open a book and find six words that end with *ch*, *sh*, or *th*.
Write the words on another sheet of paper.

Compound Connections

Directions: Cut out the cards below. Combine pairs of cards to form compound words. Glue the cards together on another sheet of paper. Then, draw a picture for each compound word.

cut ✂

grass	skate	grand
shelf	mother	corn
hopper	board	dog
book	house	pop

Think of 10 new compound words. Write each word part on its own card. Then, play a memory game, matching each pair of words.

Syllable Hunt

Directions: Write words to match each clue. Use a dictionary if needed.

1. Three animal names with two syllables.

_____ _____ _____

2. Two words with four syllables. Divide the words into syllables.

_____ _____

3. Four parts of the body with one syllable.

_____ _____ _____ _____

4. Three names with three syllables. Make sure to capitalize each name.

_____ _____ _____

5. One word with five syllables. Divide the word into syllables.

_____

6. One word with six syllables. Divide the word Into syllables.

_____

Play a syllable game. Roll a die. Say a word that has the same number of syllables as the number on the die. Score one point for each syllable. The first to reach 20 points wins.

Star-Studded Work

Directions: Write the two words that make up each contraction.

1. aren't
_____

4. he's
_____

7. they're
_____

2. she'll
_____

5. you'll
_____

8. I'm
_____

3. you're
_____

6. we're
_____

9. can't
_____

Try This!

On another sheet of paper, use each contraction above in a sentence.

Buzzing Around

Directions: Cut out the pieces of honeycomb at the bottom of the page. Pair pieces of honeycomb to form new words to match the clues. Glue each pair on the honeycomb.

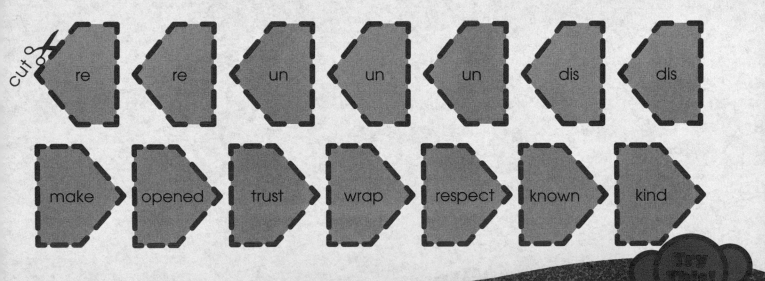

On another sheet of paper, use each new word on the honeycomb in a sentence.

Lizard Tails

Directions: Cut out the cards. Glue the suffix cards to the top of another sheet of paper. Then, glue each card under the correct suffix. Write the new word.

-er	-ful	-less
full of beauty	without color	one who teaches
_____	_____	_____
without meaning	full of doubt	one who works
_____	_____	_____
one who drives	without care	full of thought
_____	_____	_____

cut ✂

Try This!

On another sheet of paper, use each word formed above in a sentence about lizards.

23

The End

Directions: Use the suffixes **-en**, **-ment**, and **-able** to form words to complete the puzzle.

Across

1. something that governs

3. to make harder

4. able to be washed

5. something that is developed

9. something that is shipped

Down

2. able to be read

6. to make lighter

7. able to be enjoyed

8. to make tighter

On another sheet of paper, write 12 other words that have the *-able*, *-en*, or *-ment* suffix. Then, write the meaning of each word.

Synonym Clues

Directions: Write a word from the word bank that has nearly the same meaning as each clue. Use a thesaurus to help you.

academy	bandana	crate
fancy	lurch	nation
rhythm	rickety	section

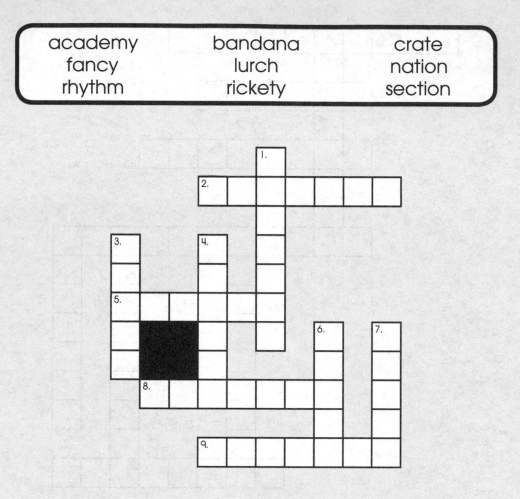

Across

2. area

5. beat

8. scarf

9. unstable

Down

1. school

3. wobble

4. country

6. box

7. elaborate

Try This!

Find an ad in a newspaper or a magazine.
On another sheet of paper, rewrite the ad using synonyms.

Fishing for Opposites

Directions: Find the pairs of antonyms. Write the words on the lines.

sharp   small   buy   big

good   weak   raw   lock

unlock   present   cooked   strong

bad   absent   dull   sell

_____ and _____   _____ and _____

_____ and _____   _____ and _____

_____ and _____   _____ and _____

_____ and _____   _____ and _____

Try This!

On another sheet of paper, write the word *dull* in large letters.
Then, cross out the word and draw pictures to illustrate the antonyms of *dull.*

Wacky Word Pairs

Directions: Answer each question with a pair of words that sound the same but have different meanings. The first one has been done for you.

1. What do you call a bald grizzly? _____a bare bear_____

2. What do you call a mare with a sore throat? _____

3. What do you call a sweet doe?_____

4. What do you call an evening with a man in shining armor?_____

5. What do you call a frail seven days? _____

6. What do you call a reasonable cost of a bus ride?_____

7. What do you call a great trick with things you walk on? _____

8. What does a small insect call his uncle's wife? _____

Try This!

On another sheet of paper, write each pair of homophones in a sentence.

Could It Happen?

Directions: Each sentence has a pair of homographs. Read the sentence and circle the correct answer.

1. Could a man with a bow bow?   yes   no

2. Could you present your friend with a present?   yes   no

3. Can a tear tear?   yes   no

4. Will a door close if you get too close?   yes   no

5. Would a doctor have wound a bandage around that wound?   yes   no

6. Could the wind wind your watch?   yes   no

7. Could lead lead the parade?   yes   no

8. Do live animals live in the wild?   yes   no

Try This!

Underline the homographs above.
Then, write the meaning of each homograph on another sheet of paper.

In Nature

Directions: Read each sentence. Then, circle the letter for the correct definition of the underlined word as it is used in the sentence.

blow	a. hit; b. breathe out hard	**box**	a. fight; b. container
buck	a. dollar (slang); b. male deer	**drum**	a. beat or pound; b. musical instrument
peer	a. one of the same age; b. look at closely	**sharp**	a. pointed; b. alert or observant

1. <u>Bucks</u> have large, strong antlers.   a   b

2. The buck's <u>sharp</u> eyes look out for danger.   a   b

3. When in danger, a buck will <u>drum</u> the ground.   a   b

4. A buck will stand on its hind legs to <u>box</u>.   a   b

5. A buck can deliver a hard <u>blow</u> with his antlers.   a   b

6. The young deer will <u>peer</u> over the tall grass.   a   b

Try This!

Create a multiple-meaning wordbook. Use a dictionary if needed.

Bookworm Part 1

Directions: Use a highlighter to highlight each entry word and its part of speech. Then, use this dictionary page to answer the questions on page 32.

absorption–organic

absorption (*n*) 1. the process of being absorbed 2. entire mind taken over by something

clay (*n*) an earthy material that is made up of minerals and is often used to make brick and pottery

compost (*n*) a mixture used for fertilizing land (*v*) to convert to compost

decompose (*v*) 1. to break down into simpler compounds 2. rot

erosion (*n*) the process of eroding

gravel (*n*) 1. sand 2. loose pieces of rock

humidity (*n*) wetness in the air

inorganic (*adj*) 1. made up of something other than plants or animals 2. artificial

microbe (*n*) germ

mineral (*n*) 1. ore 2. something that is neither animal nor vegetable

organic (*adj*) 1. produced without using chemicals 2. natural

Try This!

Look up the above words in a dictionary. On another sheet of paper, write the guide words for the page each word is on.

Bookworm Part 2

Directions: Answer the questions using the dictionary on page 31.

1. What is the quickest way to find out if the word *topsoil* will appear on this

   dictionary page? _____

2. What do the abbreviations *n, v,* and *adj* stand for? _____

3. How many definitions are given for the word *decompose*?_____

4. Write a sentence with the word *organic*.

   _____

5. Which word can be used as a noun or a verb? _____

6. What type of dictionary is this? How do you know?

   _____

7. Write two more words that could be included on this dictionary page.

   _____

8. Write two words that could not be included on this dictionary page.

   _____

Try This!

On another sheet of paper, compare and contrast a dictionary and a glossary.

Plants!

Directions: Cut out the flowerpots and glue them to the bottom of another sheet of paper. Add the correct punctuation to each sentence. Then, cut out and glue each sentence card above the correct flowerpot.

Our class did an experiment with plants

What would happen if we fed the plants juice

Wow, look at those plants grow

It was so much fun doing a science experiment

Why isn't the plant growing in the dark

Record all data carefully

Water the plants every day

Next time, we will see how plants grow with music

Declarative

Exclamatory

Interrogative

Imperative

cut

Add two more sentences to each flowerpot.

To the Moon!

Directions: Combine each pair of sentences using *and, or, but,* or *so*. Write each compound sentence on the line.

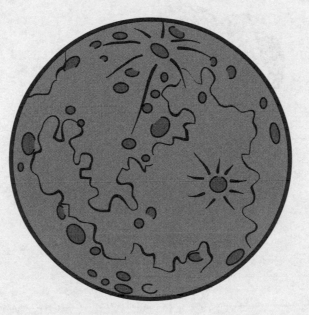

1. NASA built a spacecraft called *Apollo 11*. They launched it on July 16, 1969.

_____

2. Four days later, *Apollo 11* reached the moon. On July 20, Neil Armstrong and Buzz Aldrin walked on the moon.

_____

3. The astronauts took many pictures of the moon. They also collected 47 pounds of moon rocks.

_____

4. You can read about their moonwalk online. You can read about it in history books.

_____

Try This!

On another sheet of paper, write sentences using *and, or, but,* and *so*.

Subject Sleuth

Directions: Write the correct verb to complete each sentence.

1. In the summer, I _____ as a detective. (work, works)

2. I _____ neighborhood mysteries. (solve, solves)

3. When my friends _____ things, I help my friends find them. (lose, loses)

4. Jamie _____ things often. (lose, loses)

5. My friend Julio _____ me secret messages. (write, writes)

6. I _____ my decoder to figure them out. (use, uses)

7. I _____ my detective kit in a secret place. (keep, keeps)

8. Only my mom and dad _____ where it is. (know, knows)

Try This!

On another sheet of paper, write an advertisement for a summer job you would like to have.

Star Code

Directions: Use the code to color the verbs.

present tense = yellow

past tense = orange

future tense = blue

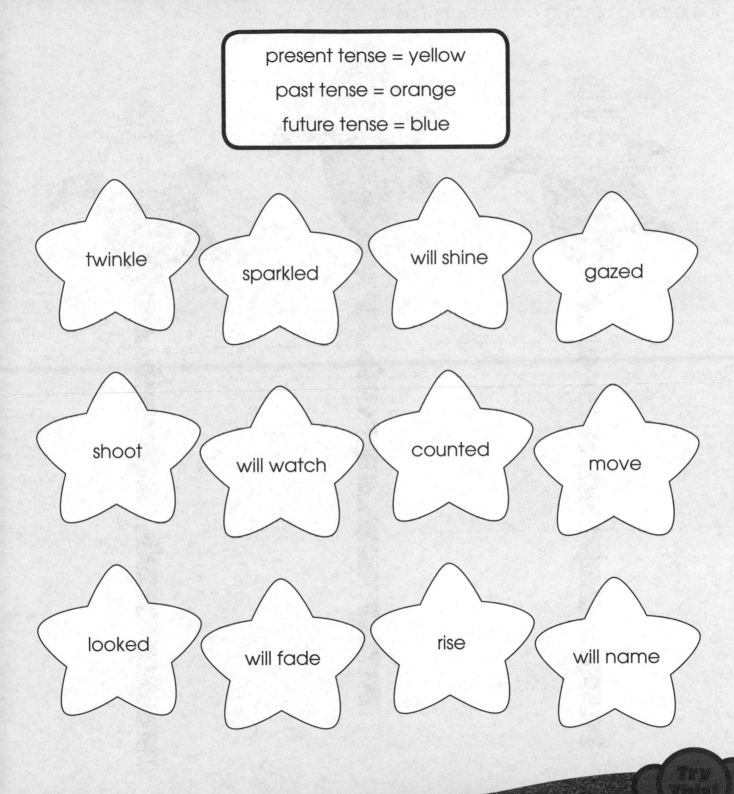

twinkle

sparkled

will shine

gazed

shoot

will watch

counted

move

looked

will fade

rise

will name

Cut out the completed stars and glue them to another sheet of paper to form a constellation.

Growing Great Pronouns Part 1

Directions: Complete each cornstalk with nouns that could be replaced with the pronoun shown on the ear of corn.

Try This!

Find a paragraph in a book.
Replace each common and proper noun with the correct pronoun.

Growing Great Pronouns Part 2

Directions: Complete each cornstalk with nouns that could be replaced with the pronoun shown on the ear of corn.

On another sheet of paper, write a story with a cornfield as the setting.
Use at least 10 pronouns in your story.

Directions: Write three adjectives to describe each of the fairy-tale characters.

knight

_____

_____

_____

princess

_____

_____

_____

queen

_____

_____

_____

king

_____

_____

_____

giant

_____

_____

_____

prince

_____

_____

_____

Try This!

On another sheet of paper, write a fairy tale using some of the words above.

One Box, Two Boxes

Directions: Write the plural form of each noun.

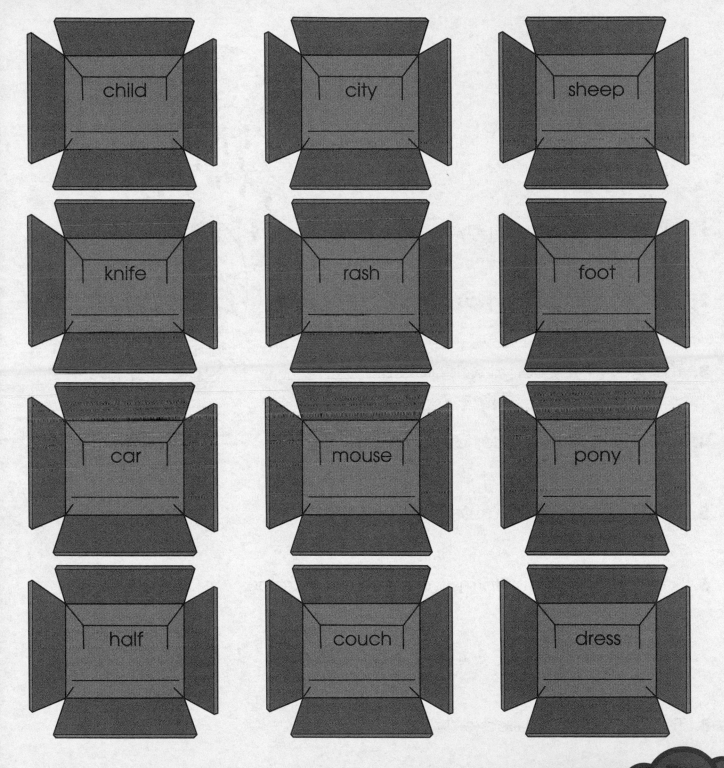

child

city

sheep

knife

rash

foot

car

mouse

pony

half

couch

dress

On another sheet of paper, use each plural noun in a sentence.

It's Raining Apostrophes!

Directions: Use a different possessive noun to complete each sentence.

1. The three _____ paws were wet.

2. The _____ room was messy.

3. The _____ pencil was broken.

4. Both _____ grades were good.

5. That is _____ house across the street.

6. Some _____ uniforms were the wrong color.

7. We saw two _____ tracks along the path.

8. The _____ mailboxes were painted red.

Try This!

On another sheet of paper, explain the difference between *dog's* and *dogs'*.

A Night on the Town

Directions: Write a proper noun for each common noun.

1. building _____

2. street _____

3. store _____

4. school _____

5. city _____

6. state _____

7. book _____

8. name _____

9. song _____

10. country _____

Try This!

In a newspaper article, circle all of the common nouns and underline all of the proper nouns.

Happy Birthday to Me!

Directions: Complete the paragraph with information about your birthday. Cross out each letter that should be capitalized. Be sure to capitalize the words that you add if needed.

My Birthday

i love my birthday! my birthday is on _____.

i will be _____ years old on my next birthday. i was born on

_____ in _____. my family celebrates

my birthday with _____.

I like to eat _____

on my birthday. On one of my birthdays, we went to _____.

I had a great time!

Try This!

On another sheet of paper, write about your best birthday. Provide a lot of details. Check your capitalization.

A Few of My Favorite Things

Directions: Provide at least three answers to each question in one complete sentence. Remember to use commas where they are needed.

1. What are some of your favorite foods?

_____

2. Who are some of your favorite friends?

_____

3. What are some of your favorite games?

_____

4. What are some of your favorite books?

_____

5. Where are some of your favorite places to go?

_____

6. What are some of your favorite toys?

_____

On another sheet of paper, write an essay about one of your favorites.
Use one of the answers above as your topic sentence.

Create a Country

Directions: Add the missing punctuation to each sentence.

1. Pilar created her own country

2. She created her country on October 29 2011

3. What would her country be like

4. What would be the law of the land

5. She wanted all citizens to be equal

6. Men women and children would have the same rights

7. All races religions and cultures would be respected

8. Everyone would live in peace

Try This!

On another sheet of paper, describe a country that you would create.
What would be the most important laws?

Snack Time!

Directions: Cut out the names of the snacks below. Glue each name under the correct snack.

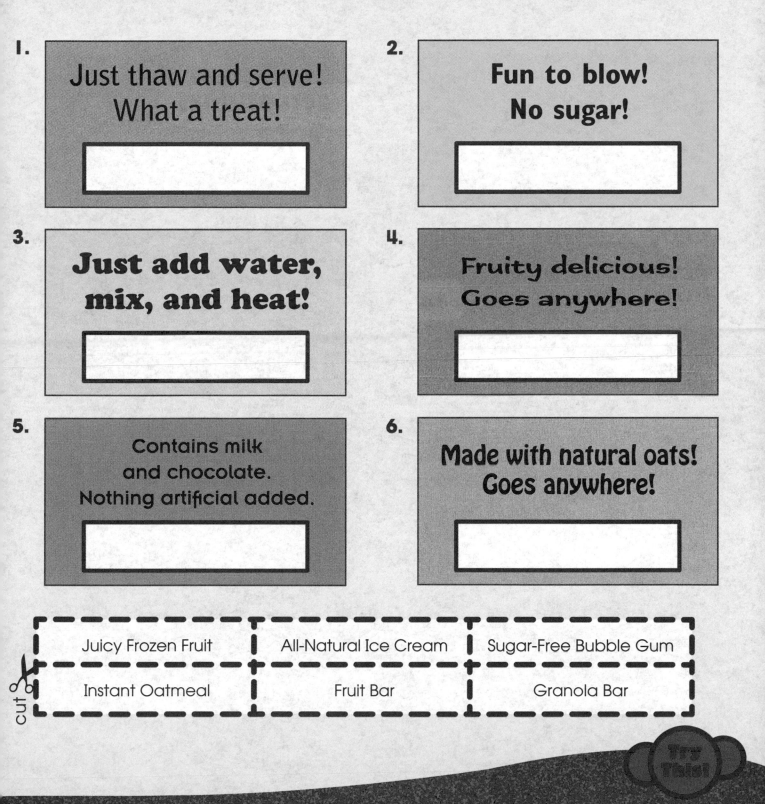

1. Just thaw and serve!
What a treat!

2. Fun to blow!
No sugar!

3. Just add water,
mix, and heat!

4. Fruity delicious!
Goes anywhere!

5. Contains milk
and chocolate.
Nothing artificial added.

6. Made with natural oats!
Goes anywhere!

cut ✂

| Juicy Frozen Fruit | All-Natural Ice Cream | Sugar-Free Bubble Gum |
| Instant Oatmeal | Fruit Bar | Granola Bar |

On another sheet of paper, write an advertisement for one of the packages shown.
Illustrate your advertisement.

How Seeds Spread

Directions: Cut out the topic sentences and glue them on another sheet of paper. Then, cut out the detail sentences and glue them under the correct topic sentence. Glue the labels to identify the topic sentences and the detail sentences.

Topic Sentences

Detail Sentences

Some seeds with spikes attach to animals' fur.	Dandelion seeds have parachutes.
Some sticky seeds attach to the feet of some animals.	Maple seeds have wings.
Animals eat seeds and move them to other locations through their waste.	The wind picks up some seeds and carries them.
The wind spreads seeds.	Animals spread seeds.

cut

On another sheet of paper, rewrite each topic sentence and its supporting details in a paragraph.

The History of Money

Directions: Cut out the sentences. Glue them in the correct order on another sheet of paper.

Then, Alexis and Emma went to the local library.

Alexis and Emma decided to research the history of money.

After the report was written, Alexis and Emma made a display.

Alexis read the book and then told Emma all about it.

Finally, the girls presented their report to the class.

Alexis and Emma's teacher gave them a research project.

Emma wrote the information in a report.

First, they looked online for important information.

There, they checked out a book called *The History of Money*.

cut

Try This!

Draw a cartoon about saving money. Your cartoon should illustrate each step in the correct order, such as earning money and putting money in a bank.

Pancake Breakfast

Directions: Read the recipe. Number the steps in the correct order.

Pancakes

Ingredients:

$\frac{3}{4}$ cup flour

1 tablespoon sugar

1 tablespoon baking powder

$\frac{1}{4}$ teaspoon salt

1 tablespoon melted butter

1 egg

$\frac{3}{4}$ cup milk

Steps:

_____ Cook the pancakes until they are lightly browned on both sides.

_____ In a small bowl, mix together melted butter, egg, and milk.

_____ Have an adult help you spoon $\frac{1}{4}$ cup of the pancake batter onto a heated skillet.

_____ In a large bowl, mix together flour, sugar, baking powder, and salt. Set aside.

_____ When bubbles start to appear in the pancake, flip it over with a spatula.

_____ Serve the pancakes with your favorite pancake topping and enjoy.

_____ Add the egg mixture to the flour mixture. Stir until it is well blended.

Try This!

On another sheet of paper, write a recipe for one of your favorite treats. Be sure to put the steps in the correct order.

Oops!

Directions: Read the story. Then, write what happened next.

The children were playing baseball in the empty lot. Mischa was at bat. She swung hard and hit the ball farther than anyone else had. The ball sailed across the lot and smashed through Mrs. Avery's window. Mischa knew Mrs. Avery would be really angry. The other kids scattered. Mischa stood looking at the broken window.

_____

_____

_____

_____

_____

_____

_____

Try This!

On another sheet of paper, write about what you would have done if you were Mischa.

What a View!

Directions: Use context clues to help you complete the passage using the words in the word bank.

astronauts	quickly	oceans
distance	data	world

Traveling in a space shuttle is fun. The _____ can see Earth

from a distance of 160 miles. Because the space shuttle orbits

Earth so _____, they also see several sunrises and sunsets in

one day.

They pass over continents and _____. It is very easy to see

the United States and the Pacific Ocean from that _____.

The space shuttle travels around the whole _____. It takes

pictures and records _____ to bring back to NASA. The

journey is incredible.

On another sheet of paper, draw a cartoon to illustrate each event in the passage above.

Complete the Story

Directions: Ask a friend to complete the story by filling in the blanks. Then, have your friend read the story to you, having you fill in the blanks. Count how many blanks you filled in the same as your friend.

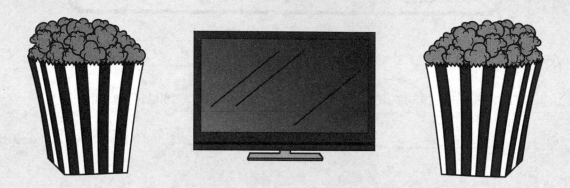

For the Love of Movies

Hannah loved movies. She would stay up until _____ to watch
(time)

them. Her favorite characters were _____ _____ and
(describing word)   (type of person)

_____ _____. One night, Hannah stayed up really late.
(describing word)   (type of person)

The next morning, when she looked into a mirror, she saw a _____
(describing word)

_____. Hannah had turned into a character in a movie. Beware!
(type of person)

Don't stay up late watching movies, or who knows what may happen!

Try This!

Fill in the blanks of the story again.
See if a friend can guess your responses.

What's Happening?

Directions: Read the story. Then, answer the questions.

Jack was uncomfortable. His new shirt was too stiff, and his tie felt tight. Mother had fussed over his hair, trying to get it to look just right. Finally, his mom smiled and said that Jack looked very handsome. Jack frowned. He didn't care about looking handsome.

Jack sat on the stool as he was told. He looked straight at the man his mother had hired. He didn't feel like smiling, but he did his best.

"Perfect!" said the man. "Let me get two more." Jack smiled two more times.

"That's it," said the man, "You're all done." The first thing Jack did was take off his tie!

1. What was Jack doing? _____

2. How does Jack feel about this event? _____

3. Who was the man who said, "Perfect!"? _____

4. Why did Jack take off his tie? _____

Try This!

On another sheet of paper, write about what you think will happen next in the story.

Field Trip!

Directions: Read the story. Then, complete the organizer.

Jeremy's class was going on a field trip to the beach. They were going to see the tide pools. They were going to study the plants and the animals that lived there.

Jeremy had just moved to Los Angeles from Colorado. He had seen snow, bears, and mountains, but he had never seen the ocean. He was very excited.

The morning of the field trip, Jeremy could not get out of bed. His throat was really sore. Every time he tried to stand up, the room spun around. His mother came in to see if he was ready. When she saw him still in bed, she knew something must be wrong. She felt his forehead. He was running a fever.

"I'm not going to see the beach today, am I?" Jeremy asked.

"Not today. But, don't worry. The ocean will be there when you feel better. We will go then," his mother said.

Setting	Theme	Character

Try This!

On another sheet of paper, make an organizer like the one above. Then, fill out the organizer to tell about a time you went on a field trip.

Feature Hunt

Directions: Choose either your science or social studies textbook. Find an example of each text feature in the book. Then, write the page number where each feature is located.

Text Feature	Page Number
table of contents	
index	
glossary	
diagram	
photograph	
chart	
vocabulary word	

Try This!

Make a bookmark that reminds you to check text features every time you read.

Waterworks

Directions: Read the diagram. Number the steps, in order, to show how water is purified.

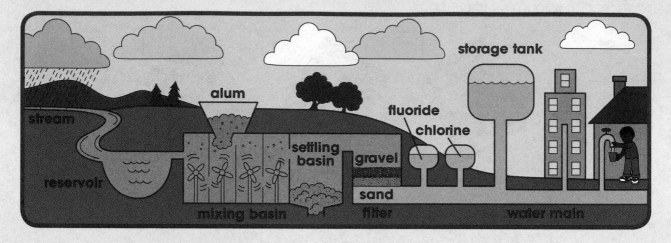

_____ The alum and dirt sink to the bottom of the settling basin.

_____ From the reservoir, water goes into a mixing basin.

_____ The clean water is stored in a large storage tank.

_____ First, raindrops fall into streams, lakes, and rivers.

_____ Water leaves the storage tank through water mains and reaches your home through your faucets.

_____ Alum is added to take the dirt out of the water.

_____ Fluoride and chlorine are added to the water.

_____ Then, the streams and rivers flow into a reservoir.

Try This!

On another sheet of paper, write the definition of *chlorine*. Use a dictionary to help you if needed. Then, make a prediction as to why chlorine is added to water.

Flower City

Directions: Read the map. Then, answer the questions.

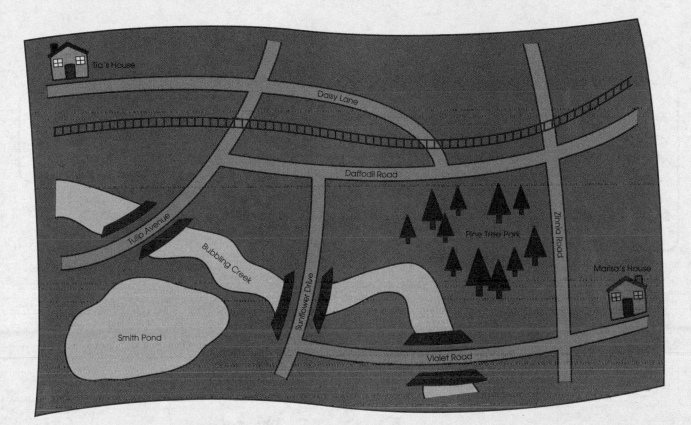

1. What three roads cross the railroad tracks? _____

2. What roads intersect both Daffodil Road and Violet Road? _____

3. How can you get across Bubbling Creek? _____

4. Give directions to get from Tia's house to Marisa's house. _____

_____

On another sheet of paper, draw and color a map of your neighborhood or an imaginary neighborhood.

Ready, Set, Draw!

Directions: Read each passage. Then, write if the passage was written to *inform*, *persuade*, or *entertain*.

Dog Tails

Where do dogs go when they need to **replace** their tails?

To **retail** stores!

_____

The Daily News

January 23

Drawing Is Easy

"If you want to learn to draw, you must be willing to practice. The more you practice, the better you will get," says a local art teacher.

_____

Try This!

On another sheet of paper, write a newspaper article that is meant to entertain.

Chirp! Chirp! Chirp!

Directions: Read each paragraph. Then, write one sentence to summarize the paragraph.

1. The baby birds were growing so quickly. Soon they would be flying. They were always hungry, so their mother flew back and forth all day long with worms and bugs for them to eat.

_____

2. Chirpy was the smallest of the three babies. He was also the bravest. He liked to jump to the edge of the nest to see his new world. The mother bird warned him to be careful. She said that he might fall from the nest.

_____

3. The mother bird flew away to get the babies their dinner. Chirpy hopped right up to the edge of the nest. Suddenly, his foot slipped. He began to fall. Luckily, the mother bird was there to nudge him safely back into the nest.

_____

Try This!

On another sheet of paper, rewrite this story from Chirpy's point of view.

Pretty Swans

Directions: Read each sentence. Write **X** in the **O** column if the sentence is an opinion. Write **X** in the **F** column if the sentence is a fact.

	O	F
1. Long ago, huge flocks of swans lived in America.		
2. Everyone loved these beautiful birds.		
3. These swans had white feathers.		
4. Swan feathers were used for writing with ink.		
5. Swan feathers were better for drawing than metal pens.		
6. A male swan is called a *cob,* and a female swan is called a *pen.*		
7. The sound a swan makes is hard on the ears.		
8. A refuge was started to protect the swans.		
9. It is wonderful to have a safe place for swans.		
10. Swans should be our national bird.		

Try This!

On another sheet of paper, draw a poster that will encourage people to save swans.

Who Said It?

Directions: Read each statement. If it is a fact, then Felipe said it. If it is an opinion, then Olivia said it. Circle the name of the person who said each statement.

1. "Eighth graders are too old to watch cartoons," complained Felipe/Olivia.

2. "A town square is part of a town," stated Felipe/Olivia.

3. "Enough rain can fall in one night to become a foot deep," explained Felipe/Olivia.

4. "Mr. Walker sells the best candy in the world," declared Felipe/Olivia.

5. "A dog is the best pet," said Felipe/Olivia.

6. "Winter is the season after autumn and before spring," stated Felipe/Olivia.

7. "Everyone likes to play in the snow," giggled Felipe/Olivia.

8. "Butter will melt on a hot pan," explained Felipe/Olivia.

Try This!

Look at the ads in a magazine or a newspaper. Do they have mostly facts, opinions, or a mix of both? On another sheet of paper, explain why you think this is so.

School Day Drama

Directions: Draw a line to connect each cause and effect.

1. Our class won the contest,

2. After our class read *Charlotte's Web*,

3. School was let out early

4. Because Jan studied hard,

5. It was raining outside,

6. Chang's alarm did not go off,

7. Our class was excited

8. Because everyone followed the rules,

A. we learned about real spiders.

B. so recess was in the gym.

C. because we were going on a field trip.

D. so we got pizza at lunch.

E. she did well on her test.

F. because of the holiday.

G. so he was late for school.

H. no one got in trouble.

Try This!

On another sheet of paper, make a list of other causes and effects you see at school.

Backyard Fun

Directions: Read each sentence. Decide if the underlined portion is the cause or the effect. Color the correct answer to reveal the path to the barbeque.

1. <u>Because it was a sunny day</u>, my family had a barbeque. (cause) (effect)

2. The food smelled good, <u>so the neighbors came over, too</u>. (cause) (effect)

3. Once the burgers finished cooking, <u>my dad put cheese on top of them.</u> (cause) (effect)

4. <u>My brother tripped</u> and spilled his food on the ground. (cause) (effect)

5. Because my brother spilled his food, <u>I couldn't stop laughing</u>. (cause) (effect)

6. Everyone was smiling <u>because we were having so much fun!</u> (cause) (effect)

7. The ants circled the picnic area <u>because they smelled food</u>. (cause) (effect)

8. Because the sun was going down, <u>we began to light candles</u>. (cause) (effect)

9. All of the kids were playing flashlight tag, <u>so the adults decided to play, too</u>. (cause) (effect)

10. <u>Because I had so much fun</u>, I will never forget that barbeque. (cause) (effect)

Try This!

On another sheet of paper, write five more cause-and-effect sentences about the barbeque.

Roller Coaster Rules

Directions: Follow the directions.

1. Color all two-syllable words blue.

2. Color all three-syllable words red.

3. Color all four-syllable words green.

4. Draw a yellow box around the words that start with the letter c.

5. Draw an orange **X** above the words that end with the letter e.

6. Draw a purple line above the words that have more than one a.

7. Circle all of the compound words in black.

8. Draw a pink **X** after the roller coaster name that you like best.

Millennium	Corkscrew	Lightning	Thunderbolt	Anaconda
Copperhead	Avalanche	Mountain	Thrill	Flashback
Speedy	Hair-Raiser	Splash	Twisted	Backlash

Try This!

Create 10 more cards with a funny roller coaster name on each.
Follow the directions above.

Our United States

Directions: Follow the directions.

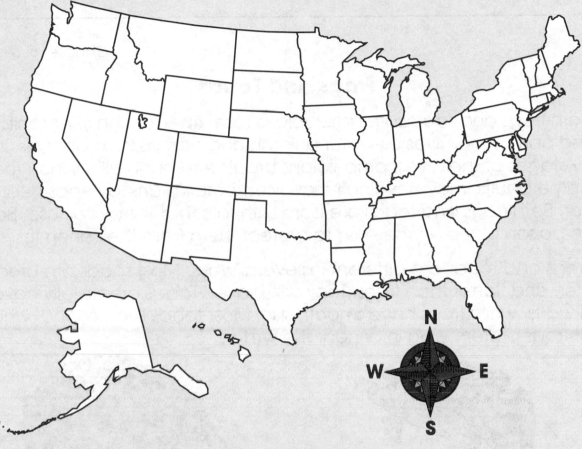

1. Write the abbreviation for your state on the state.

2. If a state is north of your state, color it blue.

3. If a state is south of your state, color it green.

4. If a state is east of your state, color it red.

5. If a state is west of your state, color it yellow.

6. Draw an **X** where four states meet at the same corner. (Hint: Four Corners in the West.)

7. Circle the two states that do not share a border with any other states.

8. Draw a star on a state that you would like to visit someday.

Try This!

On another sheet of paper, describe the route you would take to get from your state to a state you would like to visit.

About Frogs and Toads Part 1

Directions: Read the passage from a science book and answer the questions. Then, read the poem about frogs on page 71.

Chapter 5 Lesson 1

Frogs and Toads

Both frogs and toads are amphibians (am•**fib**•ee•uhns). Amphibians spend part of their lives as water animals and part as land animals. In the early stages of their lives, amphibians breathe through gills. When they become adults, they develop lungs. Most amphibians lay eggs near water. Both frogs and toads are born with tails that they later lose. Both have poison glands in their skin to protect them from their enemies.

Frogs and toads are different in several ways. Most toads are broader, darker, and flatter than frogs. Their skin is drier. Toads are usually covered with warts, while frogs have smooth skin. Most toads live on land, while most frogs prefer being in or near the water.

Frog

lives in or near water

smooth skin

Toad

darker

drier, bumpy skin

lives on land

1. Is this passage fiction or nonfiction? _____

2. What is the purpose of this passage? _____

Try This!

On another sheet of paper, draw a poster that shows how frogs and toads are alike and how they are different.

Directions: Read the poem. Then, compare this passage with the passage about frogs on page 70.

My Frog Frank

My frog Frank is the best.
He gets to stay in my room,
even at night when it is time to rest.

My frog can hop like a rabbit,
and he can swim like a duck.
But, he does have one strange habit.

My frog Frank likes to tell jokes
about fish, bears, dogs, and toads.
Yet he hardly ever croaks.

I. Is this passage fiction or nonfiction? _____

2. What is the purpose of this passage? _____

3. Which passage would you use to learn about frogs? _____

Try This!

Find a book about frogs. On another sheet of paper, draw a triple Venn diagram to compare the book to these two passages about frogs.

Directions: Read the passage and answer the questions. Use a crayon to underline each answer in the text in the color stated.

Bats

Bats are helpful animals. They are the only mammals that can fly. They are some of the best insect hunters. Bats use their mouths and ears to find mosquitoes, mayflies, and moths. They can eat more than a million insects in one night. They help control the insect population. Although most bats eat only insects, some eat fruit and the nectar of flowers. Bats also help flowers by spreading seeds.

More than 900 different kinds of bats are in the world. Some bats are small, measuring only $\frac{1}{2}$ inch (1.27 cm) long. Some bats are big. They can measure more than 16 inches (40.6 cm) long.

1. (yellow) How are bats helpful? _____

2. (blue)   How many different kinds of bats are in the world? _____

3. (red)   What do bats eat? _____

4. (green)   How large can some bats get? _____

Try This!

On a large sheet of paper, use a ruler to draw the size of the smallest bat and the size of the largest bat.

A Special Day

Directions: Read the story. Then, answer the questions by circling the answers in the text.

   Last summer, Maria and Lucy won free tickets to a water park. At the park, they floated down the lazy river ride and jumped the waves in the wave pool. They even slid down the tallest waterslide in the park! The girls ate frosty snow cones and cheesy pizza. By the end of the day, they were wet and tired, but happy. It had been a great day at the water park!

1. Who is in the story? Circle your answer in red.

2. Where did they go? Circle your answer in blue.

3. What four things did they do there? Circle your answers in green.

4. When did they go? Circle your answer in purple.

5. Why did they get to go there? Circle your answer in brown.

Try This!

On another sheet of paper, draw a map of the water park that Maria and Lucy went to. Use details from the story to help you.

A Writing Robot

Directions: Choose a topic that you want to write about and write it in the top box. Then, complete the organizer with details about the topic.

Topic

Detail

Detail

Detail

Try This!

Use the organizer to write about your favorite sport.
Then, write a paragraph about your favorite sport on another sheet of paper.

For Sale

Directions: Read the advertisements. Underline the supporting details. Cross out information that is not needed.

Skateboard for Sale

Black-and-white skateboard with royal blue wheels for sale. Like new. It was my favorite board ever. I need to sell it before I can buy in-line skates. Also comes with cool stickers. Cost is $8.00. Call 555-0123.

Bike for Sale

I am selling my favorite bike. I got it for my sixth birthday. The bike is red with white stripes. Looks like new. I took really good care of it. Comes with a light and a basket. Cost is $15.00 or best offer. Call 555-0123.

Try This!

On another sheet of paper, rewrite the advertisements, including only the important details.

Can You Sense It?

Directions: Write a story about something that happened in the school cafeteria. Use the organizer to help you use your senses to add details.

What did you see?	What did you hear?	What did you smell?

What did you taste?	What did you feel?

Try This!

On another sheet of paper, use your five senses to describe your bedroom. Then, draw a picture of your room.

Fiction vs. Nonfiction

Directions: Cut out and glue each book cover under the correct label.

Nonfiction   **vs.**   **Fiction**

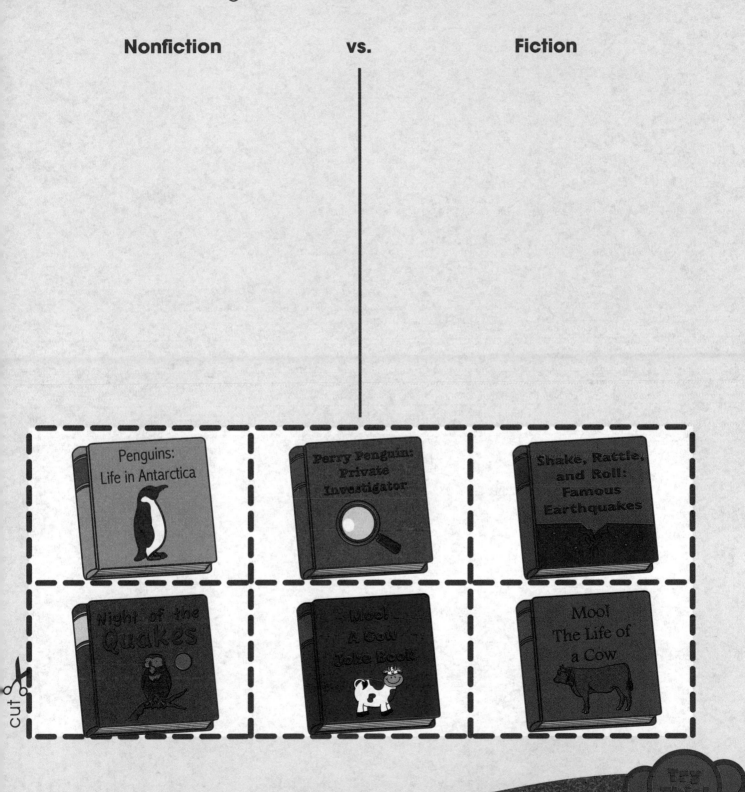

On another sheet of paper, draw a Venn diagram that compares a fiction and a nonfiction book of your choice.

Try This!

Real or Historical?

Directions: Read each description. Then, write either **realistic fiction** or **historical fiction** on the line.

1. Anna is a young girl traveling west with her family in a covered wagon. *Out West* is a book that tells about the many adventures she and her family have along the way.

_____

2. Andre and Melissa have been best friends since first grade. Can they still remain friends even after a new kid moves into the neighborhood? Read *Friends Forever?* to find out.

_____

3. *Lost* is a book about the first settlers of North Carolina. A group of people came to North Carolina and lived among the Native Americans. After several months, the whole colony disappeared.

_____

4. Kennedy Elementary School was a very fun place to be in the 1970s. Holly, Megan, and Keisha were good students. The three of them decided to start a new club at school called *The Peace Group*.

_____

Try This!

On another sheet of paper, draw a movie poster about your favorite historical fiction book.

What Did You Say?

Directions: Write some phrases that different people might say.

A phrase my teacher might say: _____

_____

A phrase my friend might say: _____

_____

A phrase my neighbor might say: _____

_____

A phrase a parent might say: _____

_____

A phrase an older brother might say: _____

_____

Try This!

On another sheet of paper, make a list of phrases your best friend says.
Then, write a story in your friend's voice.

They Win!

Directions: Read each situation. Then, write a sentence that the person might say. Be sure to use quotation marks and correct punctuation.

1. Ava's team just won the championship soccer game.

_____

2. Ava's dad is proud of the way she played the game.

_____

3. Ava's brother is happy for his sister.

_____

4. Ava's best friend likes the trophy.

_____

5. Ava feels very happy.

_____

On another sheet of paper, write a story about Ava winning the championship soccer game. Include some of the dialogue that you wrote above.

Directions: Write a story about the dog's day using transition words such as *first*, *then*, *next*, *after*, and *finally*.

_____

_____

_____

_____

_____

_____

_____

_____

Try This!

On another sheet of paper, draw a picture of what was happening with the dog right before your story started. Then, draw a picture of what happens to the dog after your story ends.

Camping Fun

Directions: Read the paragraph. Find and correct the 18 errors.

Camping can be so much fun last weekend, me and my family went camping in a park near the mountins. We took lots of stuff because we weren't sure what we would need. Dad and I set up the tents, while Mom and my brother built a campfire and make lunch. After lunch, we went swimming in the lake. Later, we went fishing my dad cot five fish! He cleaned it and cooked them over the campfire for diner. They tasted grate! After dinner, we tosted marshmallows and tell scary storys. I wasn't really afraid. Finally, we crawled inside our tents to go to sleep. It was quite except for the crickets. The next morning, we got up and starts another day of fun. I love camping?

Try this!

Create a brochure for a campsite near the Grand Canyon.

A Great Year

Directions: Read the paragraph. Find and correct the 22 errors.

Last year was alot of fun. In january, we went skiing in denver Colorado. In february, my class performed a play about the life of martin Luther king, jr. I got to play the part of dr king. In the spring, my family spent a weak at the beech. We seen two baby sharks swiming around the fishing pier! During the summer, I visited my Grandparents in Texas. I visited the space center in houston. Finally, in december, I had the best birthday ever! I got a puppy. I named him wolf because he looks like a baby wolf. Last year was relly a lot of fun. I hope next year will be even better!

Try This!

On another sheet of paper, write about a favorite thing you did with your family last year.

Take Your Pick

Directions: Circle one item in each list. Then, write a descriptive paragraph about the words you circled. Use another sheet of paper if needed.

List 1	List 2	List 3
hamster	running	at the zoo
leopard	hiding	in the bathtub
bear	stuck	under the car
parrot	sleeping	in your desk
cricket	talking	on TV

_____

_____

_____

_____

_____

_____

_____

Draw a picture of your favorite after-school snack.
Write a descriptive paragraph about it on another sheet of paper.

The Princess to the Rescue

Directions: Read the beginning of the fairy tale. Then, write two different solutions to the problem.

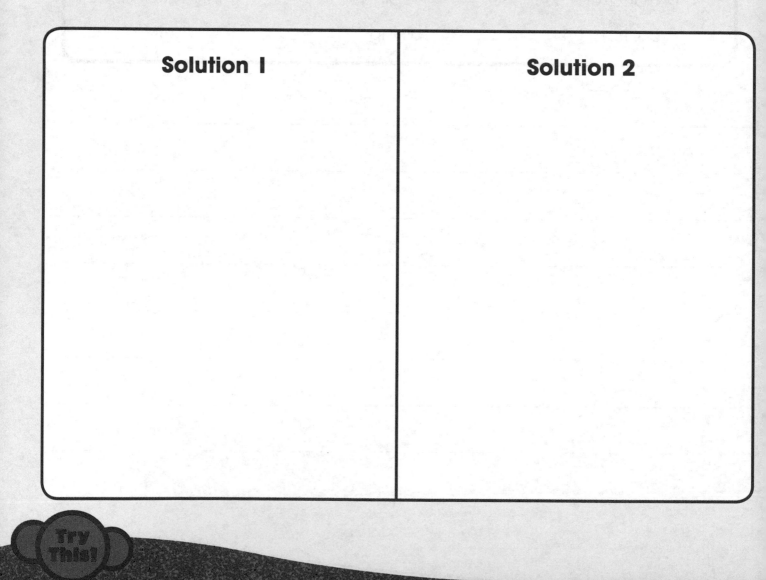

The princess had come to save the prince who was trapped in a deep hole. The princess brought only a rope, a rock, and a bucket of sand.

Solution 1	Solution 2

Try This!

Write the fairy tale from the point of view of the princess or the prince.

A School Story

Directions: Cut out the cards below. Choose one **Who**, **What**, **When**, **Where**, and **Why** card and write a story using those details.

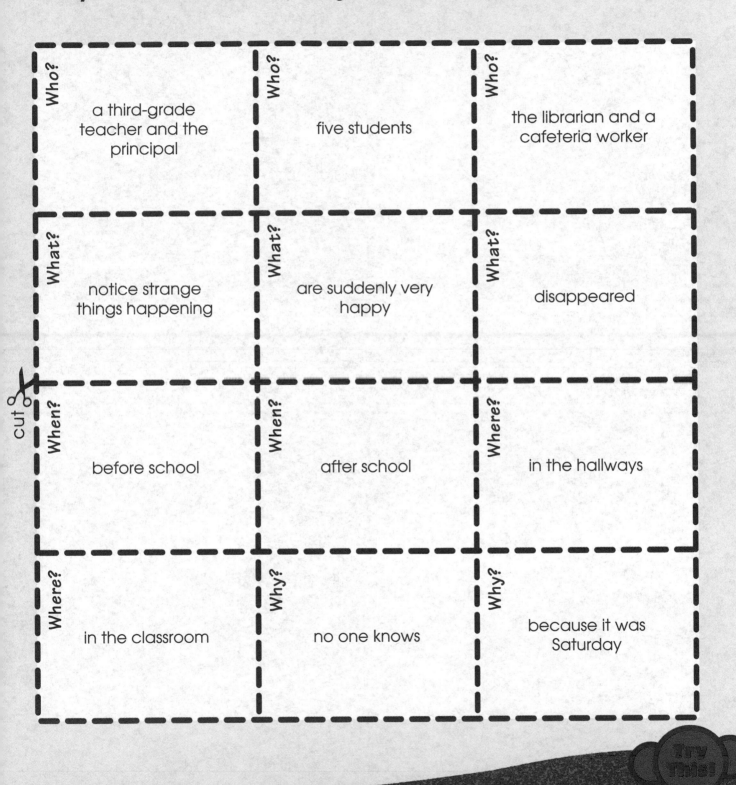

Who? a third-grade teacher and the principal

Who? five students

Who? the librarian and a cafeteria worker

What? notice strange things happening

What? are suddenly very happy

What? disappeared

When? before school

When? after school

Where? in the hallways

Where? in the classroom

Why? no one knows

Why? because it was Saturday

Write two more cards for *Who*, *What*, *When*, *Where*, and *Why*. Choose one card from each type. Write another story using the new cards.

Problems Solved!

Directions: Choose one of the problems. Write an expository paragraph explaining how you would solve the problem. Use another sheet of paper if needed.

Problem 1	Problem 2	Problem 3
how to keep from being late	how to remember to bring necessary supplies to school	how to keep track of homework assignments

_____

_____

_____

_____

_____

_____

_____

_____

_____

_____

_____

Try This!

Many inventions were created out of a need to solve a problem. Draw a picture of an invention you think might help solve one of the problems above.

Frozen Yogurt Treat

Directions: Write an expository paragraph that explains how to make your favorite frozen yogurt treat.

_____

_____

_____

_____

_____

_____

_____

_____

Try This!

On another sheet of paper, write a recipe for a cold treat.

Pretty Please?

Directions: Write three reasons why your teacher should not assign homework. Then, on another sheet of paper, write a persuasive paragraph that includes the three reasons.

Reason 1:

_____

_____

Reason 2:

_____

_____

Reason 3:

_____

_____

_____

Try This!

On another sheet of paper, write a response you think your teacher would give to your persuasive paragraph.

Two Sides to Everything

Directions: Complete the organizer to respond to the question. Then, choose a side and write a persuasive paragraph on another sheet of paper.

Should students go to school year-round?

For	Against

Try
This!

On another sheet of paper, write a persuasive paragraph for the other side of the argument.

92

Laughable Limericks

Directions: Follow the pattern to write a limerick.

> ### Limerick
> A silly poem with five lines that tells a story.
> The last words in lines 1, 2, and 5 rhyme.
> The last words in lines 3 and 4 rhyme.
>
> Example:
> There once was a girl in third grade
> who loved to sip lemonade.
> She drank it all day
> and then went to play
> while drinking the '*ade* she had made.

_____

_____

_____

_____

_____

On another sheet of paper, write another limerick and illustrate it.

Celebrating Cinquains

Directions: Follow the pattern to write a cinquain.

Cinquain

A poem with five lines shaped like a diamond

Line 1: a noun
Line 2: two adjectives describing the noun
Line 3: three *-ing* verbs describing the noun
Line 4: a phrase or a sentence about the noun
Line 5: a synonym for the noun

Example:
Big Dipper
beautiful, bright
shining, glittering, sparkling
home to the North Star
constellation

_____

_____

_____

_____

Try This!

Write a poem about the stars, the moon, or the sun.
Share it with a friend.

Dropping Digits

Directions: Write the digits **0** through **9** to answer the problems. Do not repeat digits within an answer.

1. The number that is closest to but not more than 30. _____

2. The smallest 3-digit number with all odd digits. _____

3. The number with 7 tens and 0 ones. _____

4. The greatest 3-digit number with all even digits. _____

5. The greatest 3-digit number with all odd digits. _____

6. The number that is 1 more than 323. _____

7. The number that is 10 more than 50. _____

8. The number that is 1 more than 17. _____

Try This!

On another sheet of paper, write four of your own problems similar to the ones above. Give them to a friend or a family member to solve.

Place Value Places

Directions: Complete the chart.

Place Value Chart

	thousands	hundreds	tens	ones
1. ninety-one				
2. 1,000 + 900 + 80 + 9				
3. 3,514				
4. 4,000 + 300 + 20 + 1				
5. three hundred six				
6. 1,000 + 20 + 3				
7. one thousand eight				
8. 9,150				
9. 6,000 + 100 + 3				
10. two thousand seventy				

Try This!

On another sheet of paper, use some of the numbers from above to write a narrative story about space.

Place Value Puzzle

Directions: Write each number in the puzzle.

Across

1. 3 thousands, 5 hundreds, 9 ones

3. eight thousand seven hundred fifty-four

5. one hundred sixty-two

7. seven hundred eighty-two

9. 2 hundreds, 5 tens

10. 5 ten thousands, 1 thousand, 3 hundreds, 2 tens, 4 ones

12. two

13. nine thousand six hundred four

15. seven hundred

16. eight

17. 6 ten thousands, 6 thousands, 4 hundreds, 8 tens

Down

1. three thousand seven hundred seventy-nine

2. ninety-one

3. 8 tens, 2 ones

4. 5 hundreds, 8 tens, 5 ones

6. six hundred seventy-three

8. twenty-five

9. twenty-four thousand six hundred seventy-four

11. 2 tens, 9 ones

12. two thousand one

14. four thousand

16. 8 hundreds, 6 tens, 1 one

Try This!

Color each digit in the ten thousands place yellow.

98

Step On In!

Directions: Look at the Venn diagram. Answer the questions using the numbers in the diagram. Then, label each circle correctly.

1. Write the largest number. _____

2. Write the smallest number. _____

3. Write the 5-digit number whose digit in the ten thousands place is equal to 60,000. _____

4. Write the number between 250,000 and 350,000. _____

5. Write an odd number less than 300,000 but more than 100,000. _____

6. Write an even number between 9,000 and 10,000. _____

Try This!

On another sheet of paper, write the numbers in order from smallest to largest.

There's No Comparison

Directions: Write **>**, **<**, or **=** to compare each pair of numbers. Circle the letter next to the greater number. If the numbers are equal, circle both letters. To solve the riddle, write the circled letters in order on the answer lines.

I.   **T** 759 ◯ 258 **S**   2.   **H** 161 ◯ 161 **E**

3.   **B** 25 ◯ 29 **Y**   4.   **B** 230 ◯ 320 **A**

5.   **R** 685 ◯ 594 **M**   6.   **E** 267 ◯ 267 **S**

7.   **M** 141 ◯ 139 **B**   8.   **A** 342 ◯ 324 **B**

9.   **M** 573 ◯ 753 **R**   10.   **L** 206 ◯ 208 **T**

11.   **K** 882 ◯ 822 **D**   12.   **I** 425 ◯ 254 **S**

13.   **A** 330 ◯ 338 **D**   14.   **N** 980 ◯ 995 **S**

Why do baby goats know how to compare numbers?

Answer: Because ____ ____ ____ ____   ____ ____ ____

____ ____ ____   "____ ____ ____ ____"

Try This!

Make a list of activities that involve comparing numbers.

Stack Them Up

Directions: Write the numbers in order in the place value chart. Begin with the largest number on the bottom and end with the smallest number on top.

hundreds	tens	ones

120

938

234

905

869

570

403

296

586

506

Try This!

On another sheet of paper, write the numbers in expanded form..

Rainbow Numbers

Directions: For each set of numbers, write the largest number in red. Write the second-largest number in orange. Write the third-largest number in green and the fourth-largest number in blue.

I. 5,732   921   1,240   932

_____

2. 9,834   5,685   960   4,723

_____

3. 753   4,323   1,238   1,423

_____

4. 235   3,486   8,560   4,086

_____

5. 3,483   301   235   2,463

_____

6. 4,967   3,023   2,139   587

_____

7. 932   4,672   3,984   2,164

_____

8. 256   1,236   3,710   396

_____

9. 355   6,150   9,325   4,356

_____

10. 2,356   823   908   6,346

_____

Try This!

Find 10 numbers in a newspaper or magazine.
On another sheet of paper, write them in order from least to greatest.

Every Dog Has Its Day

Directions: Round each number to the nearest ten. Match each answer with the correct letter in the key. To solve the riddle, write the letters in order on the answer lines.

1. 594 _____
2. 455 _____
3. 1,723 _____
4. 2,787 _____
5. 7,865 _____
6. 879 _____
7. 342 _____
8. 3,954 _____
9. 1,698 _____
10. 776 _____

340 = O
460 = H
590 = S
780 = E
880 = O
1,700 = L
1,720 = A
2,790 = M
3,950 = D
7,870 = P

What kind of dog likes to take a bath?

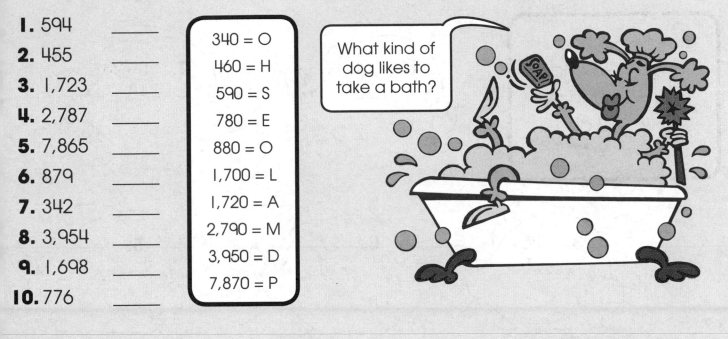

Answer: A "____ ____ ____ ____ - ____ ____ ____ ____ ____ ____"

Directions: Round each number to the nearest hundred. Match each answer with the correct letter in the key. To solve the riddle, write the letters in order on the answer lines.

11. 886 _____
12. 842 _____
13. 657 _____
14. 3,179 _____
15. 1,920 _____
16. 6,059 _____
17. 4,846 _____

700 = L
800 = U
900 = B
1,900 = D
3,200 = L
4,800 = G
6,100 = O

What kind of dog chases red objects?

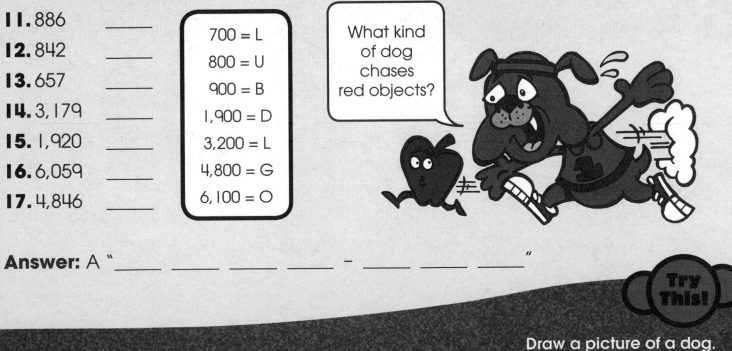

Answer: A "____ ____ ____ ____ - ____ ____ ____"

Try This!

Draw a picture of a dog.
Use the code above to write a name for your dog.

Fishy Addition

Directions: Add. Remember to regroup if needed. Use the code to color the fish.

green = 96 and 74
orange = 73 and 82
red = 35 and 52
yellow = 92 and 51
blue = 77

1.
```
  28
+ 54
  82
```

2.
```
  59
+ 18
  77
```

3.
```
  26
+ 25
  51
```

4.
```
  27
+  8
  35
```

5.
```
  67
+ 29
  96
```

6.
```
  16
+ 36
  52
```

7.
```
  34
+ 39
  73
```

8.
```
  57
+ 35
  92
```

9.
```
  19
+ 16
  35
```

10.
```
  37
+ 37
  74
```

Try This!

On another sheet of paper, write three more addition problems that have the same answer as three of the fish above. Use the code to color the fish.

Old Glory

Directions: Add. Regroup if needed. Then, solve the riddle by writing the letter that matches each answer in the correct space below.

What do the 13 stripes on the U.S. flag stand for?

1. 371 + 439 **T** 810	**3.** 146 + 587 **R** 733	**5.** 347 + 328 **H** 675	**7.** 327 + 649 **E** 976	**9.** 283 + 519 **C** 802
2. 629 + 184 **O** 813	**4.** 264 + 483 **I** 747	**6.** 382 + 249 **S** 631	**8.** 283 + 636 **N** 919	**10.** 423 + 392 **L** 815

T 810 H 675 I 747 R 733 T 810 E 976 E 976 N 919

C 802 O 813 L 815 O 813 N 919 I 747 E 976 S 631

Try This!

On another sheet of paper, draw the United States flag. In each stripe, write and solve an addition problem.

What a Web!

Directions: Solve each problem. Write the numbers of the problems that have differences of 12 in the web.

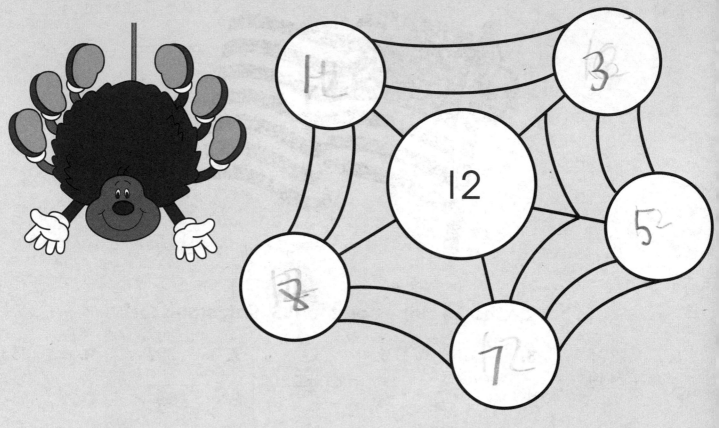

1.
$$\begin{array}{r} 59 \\ -\ 47 \\ \hline 12 \end{array}$$

2.
$$\begin{array}{r} 48 \\ -\ 26 \\ \hline 22 \end{array}$$

3.
$$\begin{array}{r} 53 \\ -\ 41 \\ \hline 12 \end{array}$$

4.
$$\begin{array}{r} 92 \\ -\ 60 \\ \hline 32 \end{array}$$

5.
$$\begin{array}{r} 44 \\ -\ 32 \\ \hline 12 \end{array}$$

6.
$$\begin{array}{r} 89 \\ -\ 75 \\ \hline 14 \end{array}$$

7.
$$\begin{array}{r} 67 \\ -\ 55 \\ \hline 12 \end{array}$$

8.
$$\begin{array}{r} 85 \\ -\ 73 \\ \hline 12 \end{array}$$

Try This!

Create a new web with the number 15 in the center.
Write five subtraction problems, each with the difference of 15.

Subtraction Superhero

Directions: Subtract. Regroup as needed.

1. 6.
    570
    − 458
    112

2. 383
    − 273
    110

3. 359
    − 259
    100

4. 359
    − 257
    102

5. 3.
    446
    − 327
    119

6. 4.
    953
    − 839
    114

7. 6.
    774
    − 658
    116

8. 7.
    384
    − 279
    105

9. 3.
    190
    − 89
    101

10. 575
    − 471
    104

11. 3.
    493
    − 386
    107

12. 8.
    751
    − 638
    113

13. 696
    − 576
    120

14. 3.
    590
    − 487
    103

15. 7.
    585
    − 476
    109

16. 6.
    372
    − 134
    238

Try This!

On another sheet of paper, write a story about a subtraction superhero.
Be sure to include solving subtraction problems as one of the superhero's greatest strengths.

107

Tic-Tac-Toe

Directions: Subtract. Regroup as needed. Draw a line through the row that
has all of the same answers.

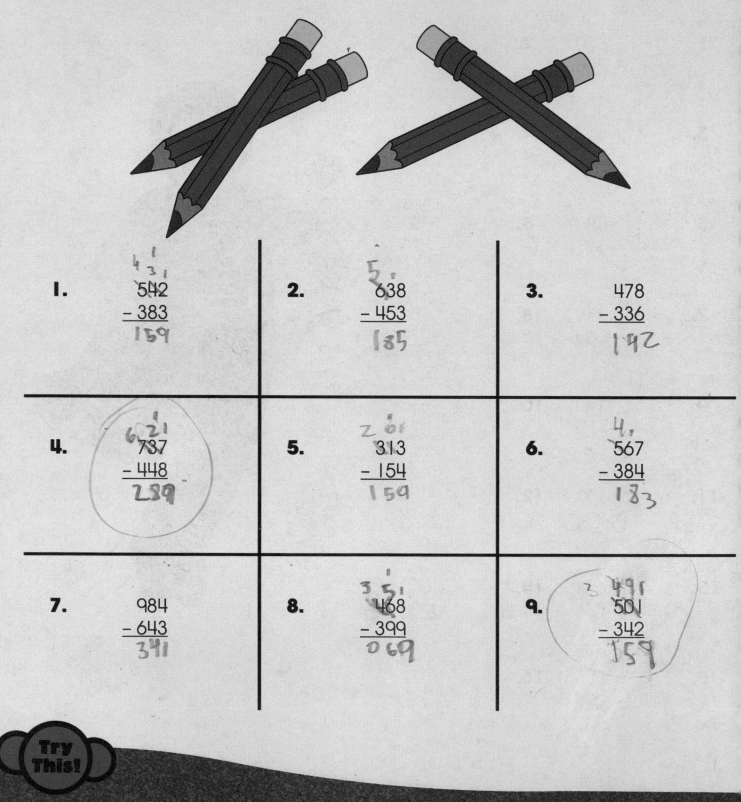

1. 542
    − 383
    159

2. 638
    − 453
    185

3. 478
    − 336
    192

4. 737
    − 448
    289

5. 313
    − 154
    159

6. 567
    − 384
    183

7. 984
    − 643
    341

8. 468
    − 399
    069

9. 501
    − 342
    159

Try This!

On another sheet of paper, create a new tic-tac-toe board with subtraction problems.
Play tic-tac-toe with a friend.

It's a Puzzler!

Directions: Add or subtract to solve the puzzle.

Across

1. 413 + 312
3. 102 + 415
4. 223 + 103
6. 131 + 253
8. 324 + 321
10. 207 + 222
12. 105 + 214
14. 315 + 400
16. 121 + 503

Down

1. 859 – 112
2. 985 – 402
3. 887 – 344
5. 789 – 583
7. 699 – 240
9. 589 – 100
11. 767 – 512
13. 497 – 321
15. 259 – 151

Try This!

On another sheet of paper, write new addition and subtraction problems that could be used to solve this puzzle.

Estimation Station

Directions: Estimate each sum or difference to the greatest place value.
Circle the correct answer.

1.   27
    + 14

A. 41   **B.** 40

C. 50   **D.** 51

2.   34
    − 28

A. 0   **B.** 10

C. 20   **D.** 12

3.   59
    + 14

A. 50   **B.** 70

C. 73   **D.** 55

4.   92
    − 56

A. 40   **B.** 36

C. 30   **D.** 20

5.   72
    + 68

A. 100   **B.** 0

C. 20   **D.** 140

6.   62
    − 48

A. 10   **B.** 14

C. 20   **D.** 24

7.   162
    + 89

A. 23   **B.** 250

C. 15   **D.** 13

8.   251
    − 143

A. 100   **B.** 300

C. 200   **D.** 250

Try This!

On another sheet of paper, write five new addition and subtraction problems.
Estimate each answer. Then, find each exact answer.

Trucking Through Addition

Directions: Use the digits **3**, **5**, **7**, or **9** to make each problem correct.

1. $836 + \boxed{}\,0 = 926$

2. $362 + 4\,\boxed{} = 409$

3. $368 + \boxed{}\,29 = 897$

4. $374 + 3\,\boxed{}\,\boxed{} = 773$

5. $8\,\boxed{}\,5 + 552 = 1{,}387$

6. $4{,}768 + 2{,}8\,\boxed{}\,4 = 7{,}662$

7. $4{,}50\,\boxed{} + 2{,}\boxed{}\,43 = 7{,}250$

8. $4{,}\boxed{}\,67 + \boxed{}{,}571 = 7{,}938$

9. $1{,}84\,\boxed{} + 6{,}7\,\boxed{}\,2 = 8{,}595$

Try This!

On another sheet of paper, explain the strategy you used to find the missing digit in each problem.

Stagecoach Code

Directions: Use inverse operations to find each missing subtrahend. Then, complete the code key.

1.
```
  5648
- *#*•
 ─────
  3223
```

2.
```
  *☺#▲
-  825
 ─────
  1323
```

3.
```
  7641
- •*#□
 ─────
  2395
```

4.
```
  7648
- ○*▲▼
 ─────
  4359
```

5.
```
  •#♦▲
- 1291
 ─────
  4117
```

6.
```
  ▲*♦▼
- 4182
 ─────
  4027
```

7.
```
  8419
- *☺▲*
 ─────
  6237
```

8.
```
  □*#▼
- 1526
 ─────
  4723
```

9.
```
  □#*▲
- 4159
 ─────
  2269
```

Code Key

*	▲	#	♦	•	☺	□	▼	○

Try This!

On another sheet of paper, create your own code and problems.
Have a friend solve the problems and crack your code.

112

Alphabet Unknowns

Directions: Replace each letter with a number to make the problem correct.

$a = ?, b = ?,$ and $x = ?$

1. $a + 7 = 12$

$a =$ _____

6. $t + 9 = 34$

$t =$ _____

2. $x + 9 = 14$

$x =$ _____

7. $51 - a = 12$

$a =$ _____

3. $s - 12 = 6$

$s =$ _____

8. $y + 13 = 25$

$y =$ _____

4. $8 + k = 18$

$k =$ _____

9. $548 - x = 123$

$x =$ _____

5. $21 + n = 29$

$n =$ _____

10. $b - 245 = 461$

$b =$ _____

Try This!

On another sheet of paper, write 10 more problems using a variable.
Then, solve for each variable.

On a Roll

Directions: Write an expression with variables to help you solve each problem.

1. Mario had some marbles. He gave 23 marbles away. He had 53 marbles left. How many marbles did he start with?

2. Mario and his friend have a total of 27 red marbles. If his friend has 18 red marbles, how many red marbles does Mario have?

3. Mario had 52 blue marbles. After he went to the store, he had twice as many blue marbles as he had before. How many blue marbles did he have after he went to the store?

4. Mario and a friend had a total of 36 marbles. Mario had 12 marbles. How many marbles did his friend have?

Try This!

On another sheet of paper, write your own word problem about Mario and his marbles. Then, challenge a friend to solve it.

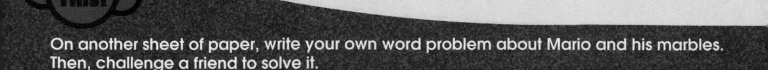

Seeing Dots

Directions: Draw a line to match each multiplication problem with its picture.

1. $3 \times 7 = 21$

2. $5 \times 5 = 25$

3. $4 \times 3 = 12$

4. $2 \times 9 = 18$

5. $6 \times 4 = 24$

6. $3 \times 5 = 15$

7. $5 \times 7 = 35$

8. $6 \times 6 = 36$

A.

B.

C.

D.

E.

F.

G.

H.

Try This!

On another sheet of paper, write eight more multiplication problems. Then, use dots to show each problem.

Top Secret

Directions: Solve each problem. Below each answer, write the letter from the code that matches. Read the coded question and write the answer in the space provided.

40	35	32	63	42	56	49	48	81	36	54	72
E	G	H	I	N	O	S	T	U	W	X	Y

9 x4	8 x4	7 x8

7 x9	7 x7

7 x7	9 x7	8 x6	6 x8	7 x9	6 x7	7 x5

7 x6	8 x5	9 x6	6 x8

8 x6	8 x7

9 x8	7 x8	9 x9

?

Answer: _____

Try This!

On another sheet of paper, create your own secret code using multiplication problems. Then, write a secret message for a friend to solve.

Practice Makes Perfect 1 to 6

Directions: Solve the multiplication problems. Then, cut out the cards and use them to study the multiplication facts.

1

1 x 1 = _____
2 x 1 = _____
3 x 1 = _____
4 x 1 = _____
5 x 1 = _____
6 x 1 = _____
7 x 1 = _____
8 x 1 = _____
9 x 1 = _____
10 x 1 = _____
11 x 1 = _____
12 x 1 = _____

3

1 x 3 = _____
2 x 3 = _____
3 x 3 = _____
4 x 3 = _____
5 x 3 = _____
6 x 3 = _____
7 x 3 = _____
8 x 3 = _____
9 x 3 = _____
10 x 3 = _____
11 x 3 = _____
12 x 3 = _____

5

1 x 5 = _____
2 x 5 = _____
3 x 5 = _____
4 x 5 = _____
5 x 5 = _____
6 x 5 = _____
7 x 5 = _____
8 x 5 = _____
9 x 5 = _____
10 x 5 = _____
11 x 5 = _____
12 x 5 = _____

2

1 x 2 = _____
2 x 2 = _____
3 x 2 = _____
4 x 2 = _____
5 x 2 = _____
6 x 2 = _____
7 x 2 = _____
8 x 2 = _____
9 x 2 = _____
10 x 2 = _____
11 x 2 = _____
12 x 2 = _____

4

1 x 4 = _____
2 x 4 = _____
3 x 4 = _____
4 x 4 = _____
5 x 4 = _____
6 x 4 = _____
7 x 4 = _____
8 x 4 = _____
9 x 4 = _____
10 x 4 = _____
11 x 4 = _____
12 x 4 = _____

6

1 x 6 = _____
2 x 6 = _____
3 x 6 = _____
4 x 6 = _____
5 x 6 = _____
6 x 6 = _____
7 x 6 = _____
8 x 6 = _____
9 x 6 = _____
10 x 6 = _____
11 x 6 = _____
12 x 6 = _____

cut

Try This!

Time yourself to see how fast you can complete the multiplication facts on this page.

Practice Makes Perfect 7 to 12

Directions: Solve the multiplication problems. Then, cut out the cards and use them to study the multiplication facts.

7	9	11
1 x 7 = _____	1 x 9 = _____	1 x 11 = _____
2 x 7 = _____	2 x 9 = _____	2 x 11 = _____
3 x 7 = _____	3 x 9 = _____	3 x 11 = _____
4 x 7 = _____	4 x 9 = _____	4 x 11 = _____
5 x 7 = _____	5 x 9 = _____	5 x 11 = _____
6 x 7 = _____	6 x 9 = _____	6 x 11 = _____
7 x 7 = _____	7 x 9 = _____	7 x 11 = _____
8 x 7 = _____	8 x 9 = _____	8 x 11 = _____
9 x 7 = _____	9 x 9 = _____	9 x 11 = _____
10 x 7 = _____	10 x 9 = _____	10 x 11 = _____
11 x 7 = _____	11 x 9 = _____	11 x 11 = _____
12 x 7 = _____	12 x 9 = _____	12 x 11 = _____

8	10	12
1 x 8 = _____	1 x 10 = _____	1 x 12 = _____
2 x 8 = _____	2 x 10 = _____	2 x 12 = _____
3 x 8 = _____	3 x 10 = _____	3 x 12 = _____
4 x 8 = _____	4 x 10 = _____	4 x 12 = _____
5 x 8 = _____	5 x 10 = _____	5 x 12 = _____
6 x 8 = _____	6 x 10 = _____	6 x 12 = _____
7 x 8 = _____	7 x 10 = _____	7 x 12 = _____
8 x 8 = _____	8 x 10 = _____	8 x 12 = _____
9 x 8 = _____	9 x 10 = _____	9 x 12 = _____
10 x 8 = _____	10 x 10 = _____	10 x 12 = _____
11 x 8 = _____	11 x 10 = _____	11 x 12 = _____
12 x 8 = _____	12 x 10 = _____	12 x 12 = _____

cut

Try This!

Write the facts that you need to practice 10 times each on another sheet of paper.

On the Farm

Directions: Solve the problems.

1. Three horses are running in a field. How many legs are there in all?

_____ horses with _____ legs each = _____ legs in all.

2. Five spiders are building webs in the barn. How many legs are there in all?

_____ spiders with _____ legs each = _____ legs in all.

3. Two grasshoppers are hiding in the grass. How many legs are there in the grass?

_____ grasshoppers with _____ legs each = _____ legs in all.

4. Four 3-legged milking stools are in the barn. How many legs are there in all?

_____ stools with _____ legs each = _____ legs in all.

5. Six cows are eating grass on the hill. How many legs are there in all?

_____ cows with _____ legs each = _____ legs in all.

6. Seven hens are laying eggs. How many legs are there in all?

_____ hens with _____ legs each = _____ in all.

Try This!

On another sheet of paper, write five new word problems using multiplication on the farm.

Down the Slide

Directions: Solve the multiplication problems.

1. 92
   x 2

2. 43
   x 2

3. 23
   x 3

4. 10
   x 8

5. 11
   x 9

6. 31
   x 4

7. 42
   x 2

8. 21
   x 7

9. 33
   x 3

10. 12
    x 4

11. 31
    x 5

12. 31
    x 6

Try This!

On another sheet of paper, write word problems for five of the problems above.

Blown Away!

Directions: Use the digits **0** through **9** to complete the multiplication problems.

1.

2	7
x	▦
5	4

2.

▦	4
x	6
8	4

3.

3	▦
x	2
7	6

4.

2	5
x	▦
7	5

5.

	3	3
	x	▦
1	3	2

6.

	1	2
	x	9
1	▦	8

7.

	2	2
	x	8
1	7	▦

8.

	3	2
	x	▦
1	6	0

9.

	1	▦
	x	9
1	7	1

10.

	2	2
	x	▦
1	5	4

On another sheet of paper, write a word problem that uses two-digit multiplication with regrouping. Challenge a friend to solve it.

Disco Dancing

Directions: Multiply. When you need to regroup, be sure to carry the number in the disco ball.

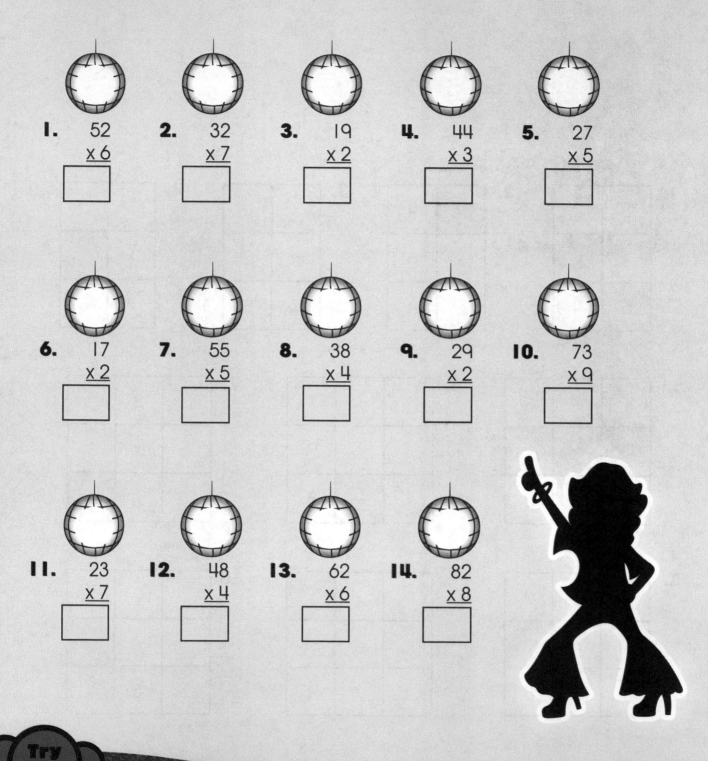

1. 52
   x 6

2. 32
   x 7

3. 19
   x 2

4. 44
   x 3

5. 27
   x 5

6. 17
   x 2

7. 55
   x 5

8. 38
   x 4

9. 29
   x 2

10. 73
   x 9

11. 23
   x 7

12. 48
   x 4

13. 62
   x 6

14. 82
   x 8

Try This!

Choose one multiplication problem from above.
Write a word problem about it on another sheet of paper.

Fun with Fleas

Directions: Draw a line to match each division problem with its picture.

1. $8 \div 2 = 4$

2. $16 \div 4 = 4$

3. $24 \div 8 = 3$

4. $36 \div 6 = 6$

5. $42 \div 6 = 7$

6. $35 \div 7 = 5$

7. $18 \div 3 = 6$

8. $28 \div 7 = 4$

A.

B.

C.

D.

E.

F.

G.

H.

Try This!

On another sheet of paper, write five more problems and pictures.

Yours and Mine

Directions: Solve the problems on each side of the page.

1. $4\overline{)12}$ $8\overline{)56}$

2. $12\overline{)48}$ $2\overline{)18}$

3. $11\overline{)77}$ $4\overline{)24}$

4. $7\overline{)14}$ $7\overline{)49}$

5. $2\overline{)20}$ $1\overline{)8}$

6. $9\overline{)63}$ $5\overline{)15}$

7. $8\overline{)24}$ $8\overline{)48}$

8. $5\overline{)45}$ $5\overline{)25}$

9. $1\overline{)11}$ $3\overline{)9}$

10. $9\overline{)27}$ $7\overline{)35}$

11. $6\overline{)18}$ $6\overline{)42}$

12. $10\overline{)120}$ $9\overline{)72}$

13. $3\overline{)21}$ $10\overline{)90}$

14. $11\overline{)88}$ $12\overline{)60}$

Try This!

On another sheet of paper, write a story about the boy on the page and how he likes to divide things into *yours* and *mine*.

We Are Family

Directions: Complete the equations.

$12 \div 3 =$ _____	$24 \div 6 =$ _____	$28 \div 7 =$ _____
$12 \div 4 =$ _____	$24 \div 4 =$ _____	$28 \div 4 =$ _____
$3 \times 4 =$ _____	$6 \times 4 =$ _____	$7 \times 4 =$ _____
$4 \times 3 =$ _____	$4 \times 6 =$ _____	$4 \times 7 =$ _____
$36 \div 9 =$ _____	$40 \div 8 =$ _____	$63 \div 7 =$ _____
$36 \div 4 =$ _____	$40 \div 5 =$ _____	$63 \div 9 =$ _____
$9 \times 4 =$ _____	$8 \times 5 =$ _____	$7 \times 9 =$ _____
$4 \times 9 =$ _____	$5 \times 8 =$ _____	$9 \times 7 =$ _____
$35 \div 7 =$ _____	$54 \div 6 =$ _____	$32 \div 8 =$ _____
$35 \div 5 =$ _____	$54 \div 9 =$ _____	$32 \div 4 =$ _____
$7 \times 5 =$ _____	$9 \times 6 =$ _____	$8 \times 4 =$ _____
$5 \times 7 =$ _____	$6 \times 9 =$ _____	$4 \times 8 =$ _____

Try This!

Write a fact family using the numbers 7, 6, and 42.

Make It Fair

Directions: Read each problem and draw a picture to show what is happening. Then, solve the problem.

I. Tony has 12 cookies. There are 6 children. How many cookies will each child get?

2. The pet shelter received a donation of 24 dog biscuits. Eight dogs are at the shelter. How many biscuits should each dog get?

3. Renee is making 5 pizzas. She has 25 pieces of pepperoni to divide between the pizzas. How many pieces of pepperoni should go on each pizza?

4. Mr. Ormand has 18 books to place on 3 shelves. He wants to put the same number of books on each shelf. How many books should he put on each shelf?

Try This!

On another sheet of paper, list at least five problems you would need to solve using division.

Hop to It!

Directions: Solve the division problems.

1. 5)65   2. 4)44   3. 8)96   4. 7)91

5. 3)54   6. 2)66   7. 6)78   8. 9)90

9. 3)45   10. 4)64   11. 5)95   12. 3)93

13. 2)84   14. 3)66   15. 6)84   16. 5)85

Try This!

On another sheet of paper, make a list of times outside of school when it may be helpful to
know how to divide.

Take a Spin

Directions: Turn the wheel and solve the division problems. Use *r* to show the remainders.

1. 86 ÷ 9
2. 30 ÷ 7
3. 65 ÷ 4
4. 37 ÷ 2
5. 40 ÷ 3
6. 72 ÷ 5
7. 49 ÷ 3
8. 55 ÷ 2
9. 73 ÷ 6
10. 82 ÷ 7
11. 66 ÷ 4
12. 54 ÷ 5

Try This!

On another sheet of paper, write and solve 10 additional division problems.

Cool!

Directions: To solve the riddle below, match the numbers with remainders and write the letters on the lines.

E. 5)37   T. 3)28   D. 5)18   S. 6)46

I. 4)31   B. 3)37   U. 8)43   H. 10)32

A. 12)74   N. 4)25   R. 8)87   G. 6)14

Why do teachers wear sunglasses?

___ ___ ___ C ___ ___ ___ ___
12 r1   7 r2   6 r2   5 r3   7 r4   7 r2

___ ___ ___ ___ ___
9 r1   3 r2   7 r2   7 r3   10 r7

___ ___ ___ ___ ___ ___ ___ ___
7 r4   9 r1   5 r3   3 r3   7 r2   6 r1   9 r1   7 r4

___ ___ ___
6 r2   10 r7   7 r2

___ O
7 r4

___ R ___ ___ ___ ___!
12 r1   7 r3   2 r2   3 r2   9 r1

Write five more division problems that will have remainders.
Challenge a friend to solve them correctly.

Try This!

Popping Problems

Directions: Read each problem and write a number sentence to show what is happening. Then, solve the problem.

1. Stephen had 24 bags of popcorn to sell at the snack bar. He sold all of the popcorn to six customers. If each customer bought the same number of bags, how many bags did each customer buy?

2. Philip sold 69 buckets of popcorn. He worked for three weeks and sold the same amount each week. How many buckets of popcorn did he sell each week?

3. Brandon sold 88 buckets of popcorn in two weeks. If he sold the same amount each week, how many buckets of popcorn did he sell each week?

4. Kennedy popped 75 cups of popcorn in 3 days. If she popped the same number of cups each day, how many cups did she pop each day?

5. Ana popped 52 cups of popcorn in two days. Who popped more cups of popcorn each day, Kennedy or Ana?

6. Cody popped 76 cups of popcorn in four days. Did she pop more or fewer cups of popcorn each day than Kennedy and Ana?

Try This!

Choose one of the problems above and draw a picture to show the problem and how you solved it.

Operation Options

Directions: Write the correct symbol in each oval. Use **+**, **-**, **x**, or **÷** .

1. 7 ◯ 8 = 56

2. 54 ◯ 9 = 6

3. 36 ◯ 5 = 31

4. 12 ◯ 6 = 18

5. 72 ◯ 7 = 65

6. 18 ◯ 5 = 23

7. 40 ◯ 2 = 38

8. 8 ◯ 8 = 64

9. 62 ◯ 25 = 37

10. 48 ◯ 6 = 8

11. 32 ◯ 4 = 8

12. 6 ◯ 7 = 42

13. 72 ◯ 8 = 9

14. 45 ◯ 29 = 16

Try This!

Write word problems to go along with five problems above.

Money Bags

Directions: Read the value of the coins. Write the total on each money bag.

1. 1 quarter
1 dime
1 nickel
2 pennies

2. 2 quarters
1 dime
1 nickel
1 penny

3. 3 quarters
2 dimes
2 pennies

4. 1 quarter
3 dimes
2 nickels
8 pennies

5. 2 quarters
2 dimes
3 nickels
3 pennies

6. 1 quarter
3 dimes
4 nickels
5 pennies

Try This!

On another sheet of paper, write different ways of combining coins to equal 15 cents.

The Fewest Coins

Directions: Write the amount shown using the least number of coins to make that amount.

	Amount	Quarters	Dimes	Nickels	Pennies
1.	$0.76				
2.	$0.45				
3.	$0.98				
4.	$0.40				
5.	$0.84				
6.	$0.62				
7.	$1.42				
8.	$1.68				

Try This!

On another sheet of paper, make another chart like the one above.
Then, figure out the most number of coins needed to make each amount.

Directions: Add.

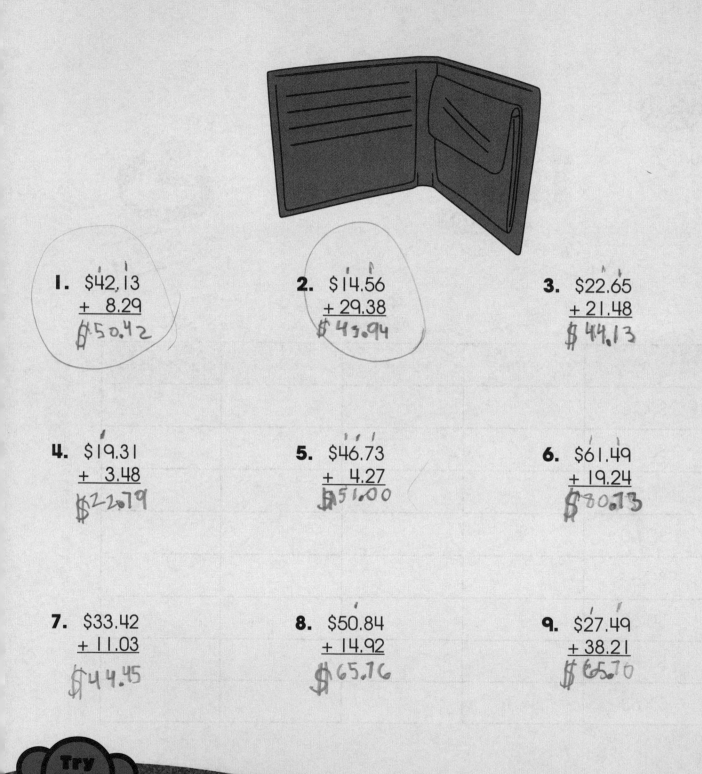

1. $42.13
+ 8.29
$50.42

2. $14.56
+ 29.38
$43.94

3. $22.65
+ 21.48
$ 44.13

4. $19.31
+ 3.48
$22.79

5. $46.73
+ 4.27
$51.00

6. $61.49
+ 19.24
$80.73

7. $33.42
+ 11.03
$44.45

8. $50.84
+ 14.92
$65.76

9. $27.49
+ 38.21
$65.70

Try This!

Imagine that you found a receipt that has the amounts $15.95, $2.50, $12.00, and $7.25. Write what you would have bought with each amount and add to find the total cost.

You Had, You Spent

Directions: Read and solve the problems.

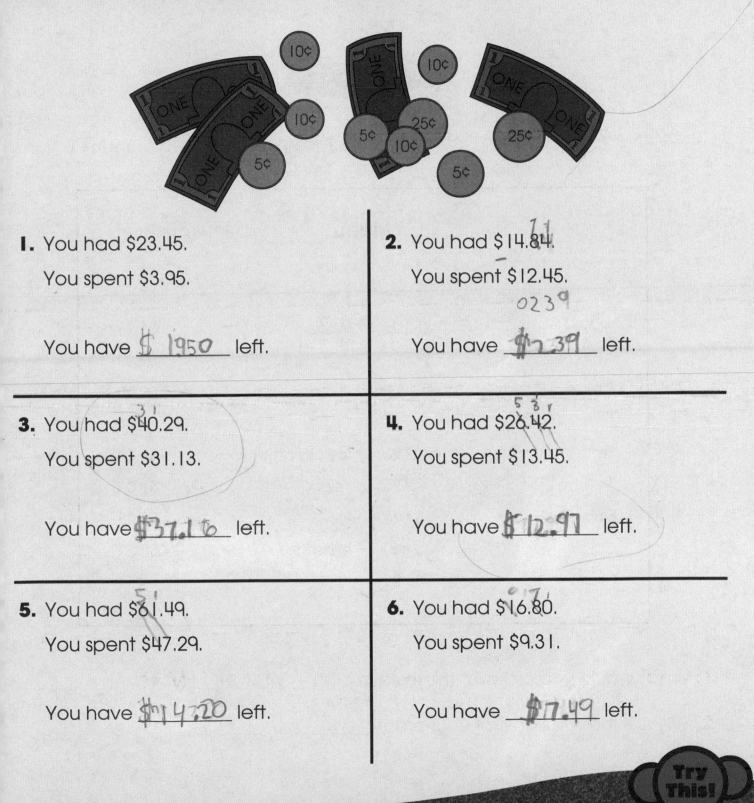

1. You had $23.45.

You spent $3.95.

You have $ 1950 left.

2. You had $14.84.

You spent $12.45.

0239

You have $2.39 left.

3. You had $40.29.

You spent $31.13.

You have $37.16 left.

4. You had $26.42.

You spent $13.45.

You have $12.97 left.

5. You had $61.49.

You spent $47.29.

You have $14.20 left.

6. You had $16.80.

You spent $9.31.

You have $7.49 left.

Choose one of the problems above. On another sheet of paper, write a story that tells about the money you had, how you spent it, and how much you have left.

Order Up! Part 1

Directions: Read the menu. Then, answer the questions.

Menu

Chicken Nuggets	$1.95		
PB&J Sandwich	$2.50	Milk	$1.25
Hamburger	$3.25	Water	$1.25
(with cheese add $0.75)		Soft Drink	$2.00
Chicken Sandwich	$4.15	Juice	$2.25
Soup	$2.25	Ice Cream	$3.75
Salad	$2.25	Yogurt	$2.00
Fruit	$1.75	Pie	$3.25
Chips	$2.00	Milkshake	$2.25
Fries	$3.25		

1. What would you order at this restaurant? _Chicken Nuggets_

2. What is the total cost of your order? _$5.45_

Try This!

On another sheet of paper, write an order to feed everyone in your family.
Then, add to find the total cost of the meal.

Order Up! Part 2

Directions: Read each order. Then, use the menu on page 138 to figure out
how much each meal cost.

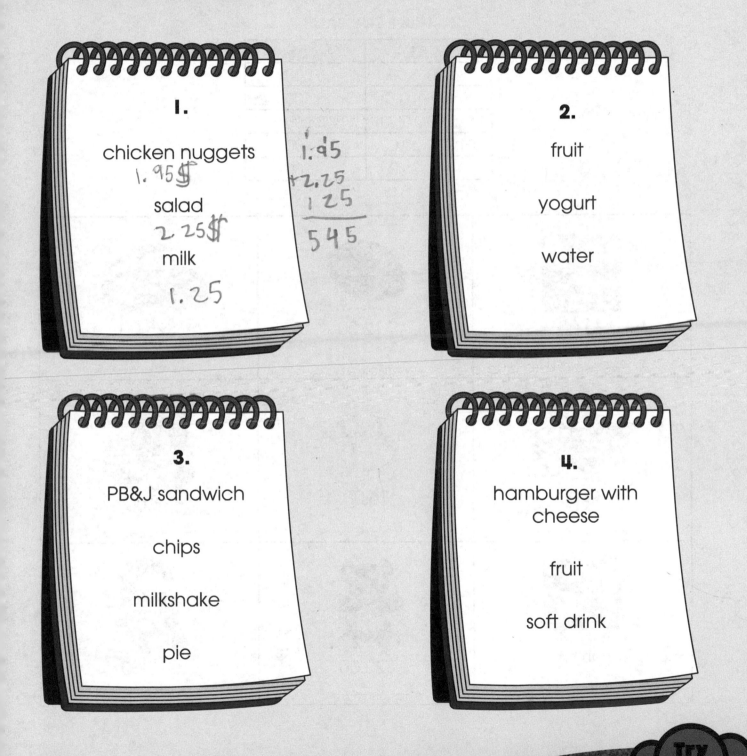

1.

chicken nuggets   1.95

1.95 $

salad   +2.25

2 25 $ 1 25

milk   ———

1.25   545

2.

fruit

yogurt

water

3.

PB&J sandwich

chips

milkshake

pie

4.

hamburger with
cheese

fruit

soft drink

Try
This!

How much change would you get back from each order above if you had $15.75 to start
with? Solve the problems on another sheet of paper.

Big Discount

Directions: Read the flyer. Then, figure out the new sale price of each item.

HUGE TOY SALE!

Original Price	Discount
$3.00–5.00	$1.00
$6.00–10.00	$2.00
$11.00–15.00	$3.00
$16.00–20.00	$4.00
$21.00–25.00	$5.00

$3.00
_____

$12.00
_____

$25.00
_____

$8.00
_____

$6.00
_____

$5.00
_____

$24.00
_____

$22.00
_____

$15.00
_____

Try This!

If you were to buy all of the toys, how much would they cost in all at regular price? How much would they cost in all with the discount? Show your work on another sheet of paper.

Parts of a Whole

Directions: Color to show the fractions.

1.
$$\frac{2}{3}$$

2.
$$\frac{1}{5}$$

3.
$$\frac{4}{6}$$

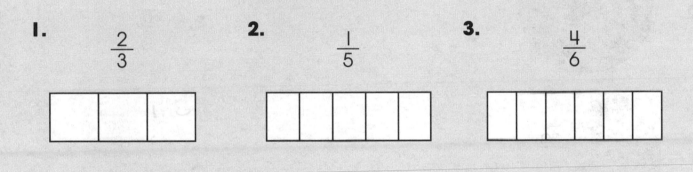

4.
$$\frac{1}{2}$$

5.
$$\frac{1}{4}$$

6.
$$\frac{3}{3}$$

7.
$$\frac{3}{5}$$

8.
$$\frac{3}{4}$$

9.
$$\frac{5}{6}$$

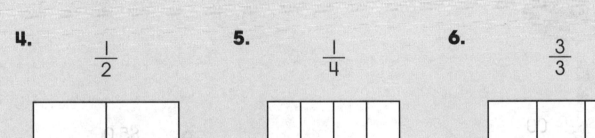

Try This!

On another sheet of paper, draw another shape to illustrate each fraction above.

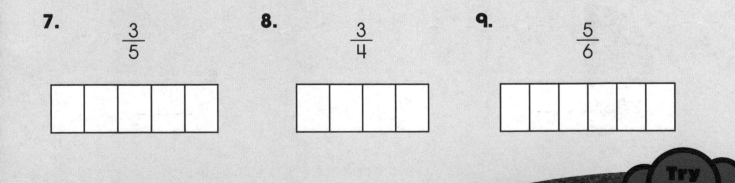

Pizza Parlor

Directions: Draw a line to match the amount of each pizza to its fraction.

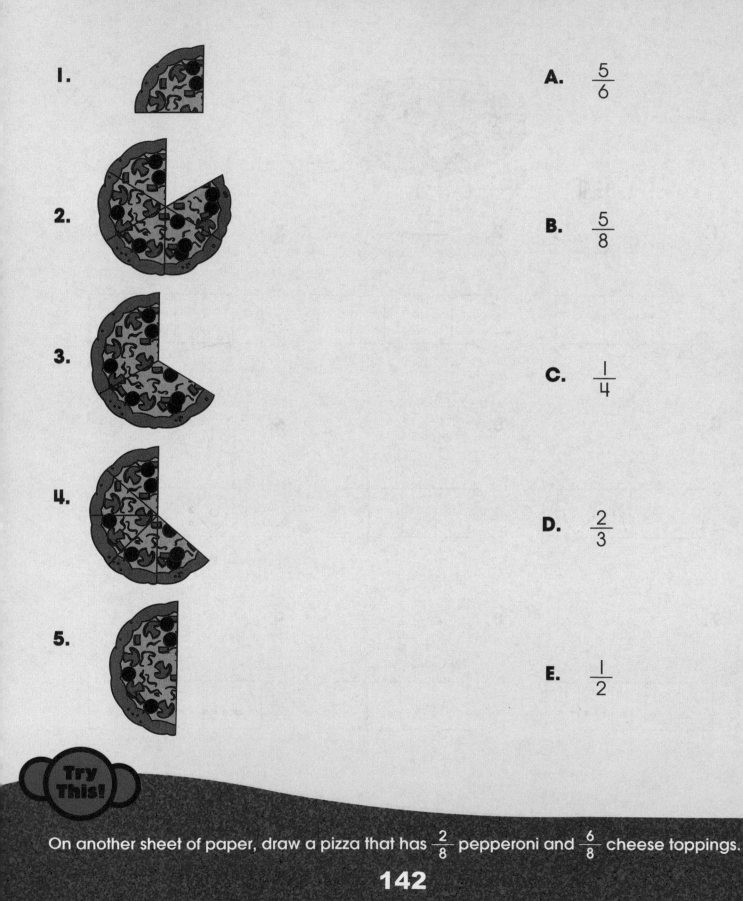

1.

2.

3.

4.

5.

A. $\dfrac{5}{6}$

B. $\dfrac{5}{8}$

C. $\dfrac{1}{4}$

D. $\dfrac{2}{3}$

E. $\dfrac{1}{2}$

Try This!

On another sheet of paper, draw a pizza that has $\dfrac{2}{8}$ pepperoni and $\dfrac{6}{8}$ cheese toppings.

Cheesy!

Directions: Color the fraction on the cheese. Then, cut out the cards. Glue each mouse to the top of a sheet of paper. Glue each equivalent fraction below the correct mouse.

On another sheet of paper, write 10 different fractions equivalent to $\frac{1}{2}$. What pattern do you see?

Which Is More?

Directions: Color the fractions and then compare. Use **>**, **<**, or **=** to make each number sentence true.

I.

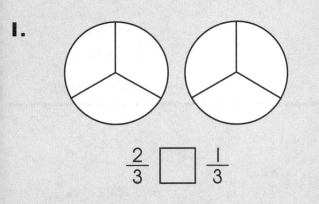

$$\frac{2}{3} \ \square \ \frac{1}{3}$$

2.

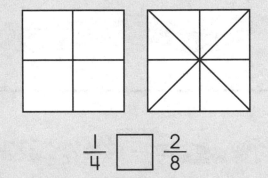

$$\frac{1}{4} \ \square \ \frac{2}{8}$$

3. **4.**

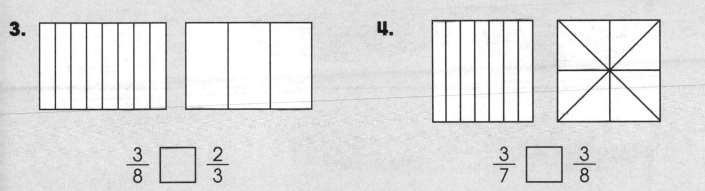

$$\frac{3}{8} \ \square \ \frac{2}{3}$$

$$\frac{3}{7} \ \square \ \frac{3}{8}$$

5. **6.**

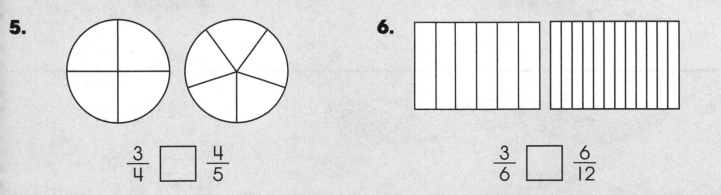

$$\frac{3}{4} \ \square \ \frac{4}{5}$$

$$\frac{3}{6} \ \square \ \frac{6}{12}$$

Try This!

Draw a Venn diagram. Label one circle "More Than $\frac{1}{2}$" and the other "Less Than $\frac{1}{2}$." Place these fractions in the diagram: $\frac{3}{6}, \frac{5}{8}, \frac{7}{9}, \frac{2}{4}, \frac{6}{7}, \frac{4}{8}, \frac{3}{4}, \frac{1}{3}, \frac{2}{5}$.

Inchworms?

Directions: Measure the worms. Write the length of each worm to the closest $\frac{1}{2}$ inch and centimeter.

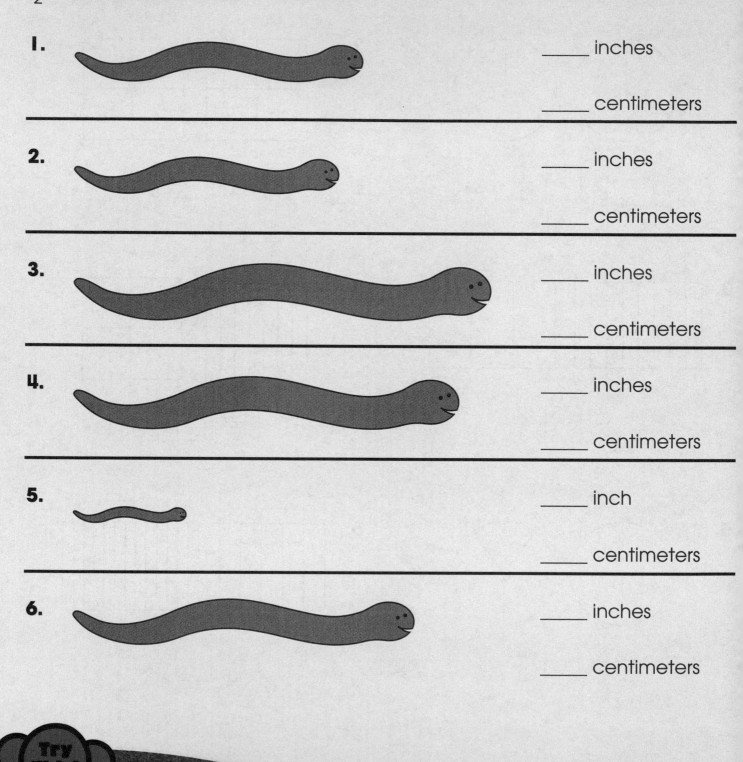

1. _____ inches

   _____ centimeters

2. _____ inches

   _____ centimeters

3. _____ inches

   _____ centimeters

4. _____ inches

   _____ centimeters

5. _____ inch

   _____ centimeters

6. _____ inches

   _____ centimeters

Try This!

On another sheet of paper, draw five more worms and measure each one. Write the measurements in inches and centimeters.

Measurement Matters

Directions: Read the conversions. Then, solve the problems.

> 1 foot = 12 inches
>
> 1 yard = 3 feet or 36 inches

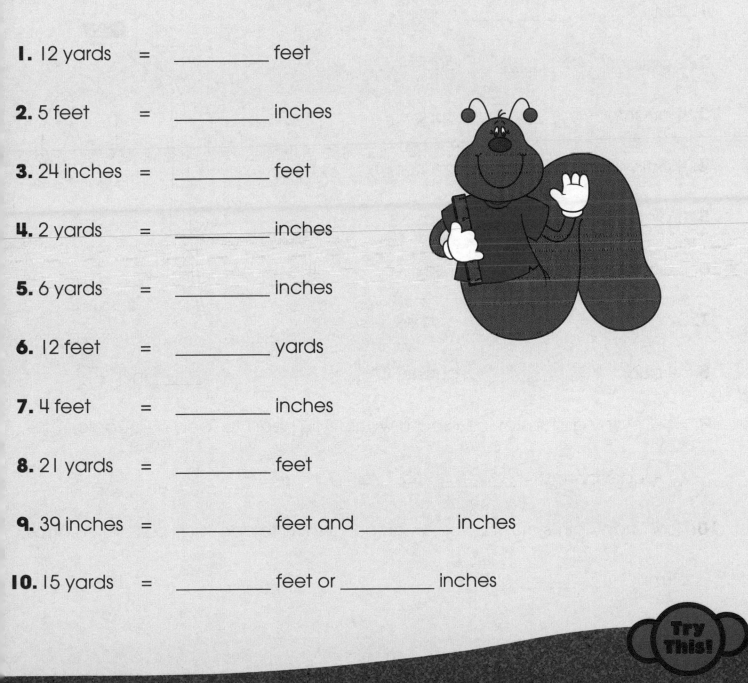

1. 12 yards = _____ feet

2. 5 feet = _____ inches

3. 24 inches = _____ feet

4. 2 yards = _____ inches

5. 6 yards = _____ inches

6. 12 feet = _____ yards

7. 4 feet = _____ inches

8. 21 yards = _____ feet

9. 39 inches = _____ feet and _____ inches

10. 15 yards = _____ feet or _____ inches

Try This!

On another sheet of paper, write three things you would measure in inches, three things you would measure in feet, and three things you would measure in yards.

In the Kitchen

Directions: Read the conversions. Then, solve the problems.

> 1 pint = 2 cups
> 1 quart = 2 pints or 4 cups
> 1 gallon = 4 quarts, 8 pints, or 16 cups

1. 2 pints = _____ cups

2. 2 gallons = _____ quarts

3. 4 quarts = _____ cups

4. 4 gallons = _____ pints

5. 3 pints = _____ cups

6. 3 quarts = _____ cups

7. 32 cups = _____ gallons

8. 64 cups = _____ quarts

9. How many gallons of ice cream would you need to feed 64 people

$\frac{1}{2}$-cup servings? _____

10. How many pints of milk would you need for a recipe that calls for 16 cups

of milk? _____

Try This!

Make a poster that illustrates liquid measurement equivalents.
Use pictures, not words.

Measure Up

Directions: Under each picture, write the unit of measurement (ounces, pounds, or tons) that the object would be measured in.

> 16 ounces = a pound
> 2,000 pounds = a ton

1.

2.

3.

4.

5.

6.

7.

8.

9.

Try This!

On another sheet of paper, for each unit of measurement (ounces, pounds, and tons), draw a picture of an object measured in that unit.

Experiment a Little!

Directions: Read the conversions. Then, draw a line to match each weight with its equivalent.

16 ounces = 1 pound
2,000 pounds = 1 ton
1,000 grams = 1 kilogram

1. 16 ounces

2. 4,000 pounds

3. 3 kilograms

4. 1 ton

5. 80,000 ounces

6. 10,000 grams

7. 8 pounds

8. $\frac{1}{2}$ kilogram

A. 3,000 grams

B. 1 pound

C. 5,000 pounds

D. 128 ounces

E. 500 grams

F. 10 kilograms

G. 32,000 ounces

H. 2 tons

Try This!

Write a letter to your senator to explain why you think the United States should switch to measuring mass in grams and kilograms.

Bubbles, Bubbles

Directions: Solve the problems. Color the correct answers. Cross out the incorrect answers.

1. Alex blew bubbles in his driveway. The bubble that traveled the farthest flew 5 feet. How many inches did it travel?

(50 ft.) (60 in.) (12 in.) (60 ft.)

2. Alex got a gallon of bubbles for his birthday. How many quarts did he have?

(12) (8) (4) (1)

3. If Alex blows bubbles 3 feet into the air and then the wind blows them 24 inches higher, how high did the bubbles blow in all?

(5 ft.) (27 ft.) (70 in.) (50 in.)

4. Alex had one gallon of bubbles. He thinks that if he pours out two quarts of bubbles, he will have four pints left. Is he right?

(yes) (no)

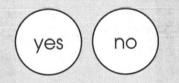

Try This!

On another sheet of paper, write your own measurement problem about Alex and his bubbles. Then, solve the problem.

Today's Weather

Directions: Label each thermometer to match the temperature given.

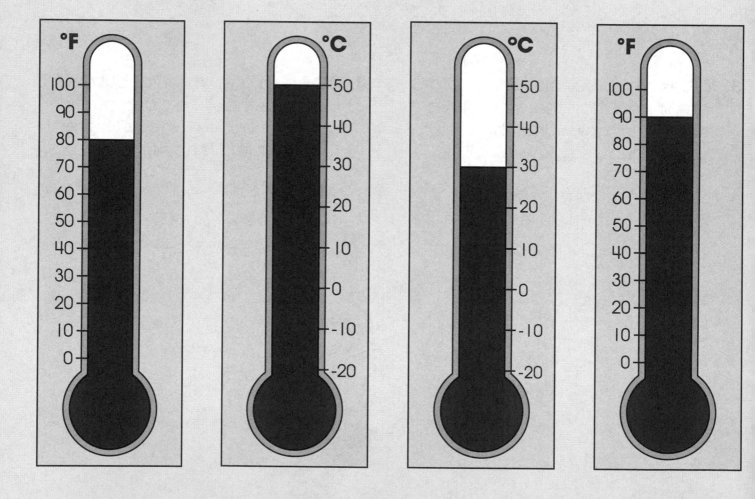

On another sheet of paper, draw and label your own thermometer.
Be sure to include both Celsius and Fahrenheit.

Got the Time?

Directions: Write the time on each clock.

1.

_____

2.

_____

3.

_____

4.

_____

5.

_____

6.

_____

7.

_____

8.

_____

9.

_____

Think about your daily schedule. On another sheet of paper, write the times of six events. Then, draw a clock to show each time.

153

Try This!

All Hands on Deck

Directions: Read and solve the problems.

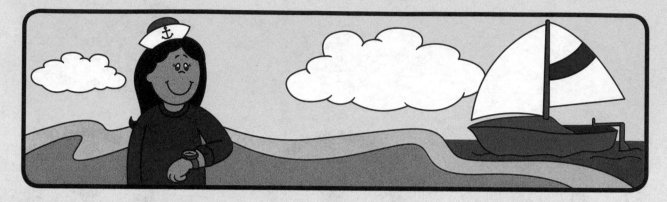

1. Brooke woke up at 6:05 A.M. She had 55 minutes to report for duty. What time did Brooke need to arrive for duty?

2. Brooke's shift started at 7:00 A.M. She was scheduled to work 5 $\frac{1}{2}$ hours. What time would her shift be over?

3. Brooke arrived at the gym to work out at 1:15 P.M. Her workout took 45 minutes. What time was Brooke done at the gym?

4. Brooke met friends for dinner at 7:00 P.M. She spent 3 hours and 20 minutes with her friends. What time did she leave her friends?

5. Brooke called her sister at 8:10 P.M. They talked for 47 minutes. What time did Brooke get off the phone?

6. Brooke went to bed at 10:00 P.M. She woke up the next morning at 6:00 A.M. How many hours did she sleep?

Try This!

On another sheet of paper, write six time problems about your day. Have a friend solve the problems.

Take Your Time

Directions: Write the time shown on each clock. Then, find the time elapsed between each pair of times.

1.

_____   _____

Elapsed Time: _____

2.

_____   _____

Elapsed Time: _____

3.

_____   _____

Elapsed Time: _____

4.

_____   _____

Elapsed Time: _____

5.

_____   _____

Elapsed Time: _____

6.

_____   _____

Elapsed Time: _____

Try This!

Think of an activity you do. Write the time you start the activity and the time the activity ends. How much time does the activity take?

Dive In!

Directions: Find the area of each shape. (Each square equals 1.)

1.

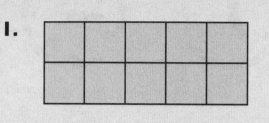

Area =_____

2.

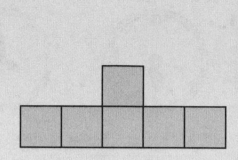

Area =_____

3.

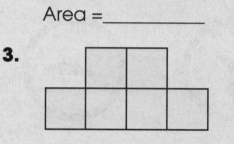

Area =_____

4.

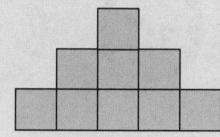

Area =_____

5.

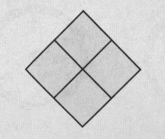

Area =_____

6.

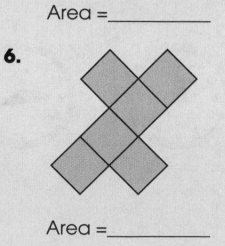

Area =_____

Try This!

On a sheet of grid paper, draw four more shapes and find the area of each shape.

Fenced In

Directions: Find the perimeter of each shape.

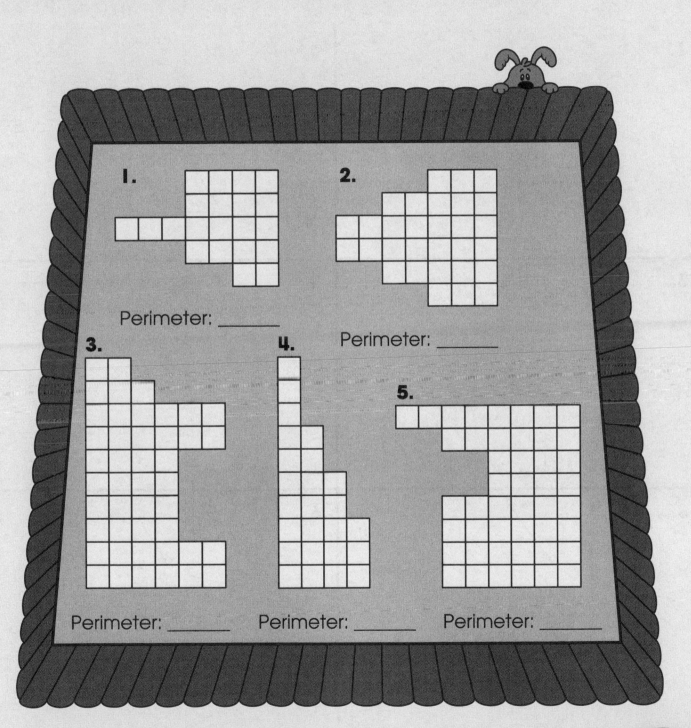

1. Perimeter: _____

2. Perimeter: _____

3. Perimeter: _____

4. Perimeter: _____

5. Perimeter: _____

Try This!

On a sheet of grid paper, draw three more shapes.
Find the perimeter of each shape.

Down the Middle

Directions: Draw each matching part to make the object symmetrical.

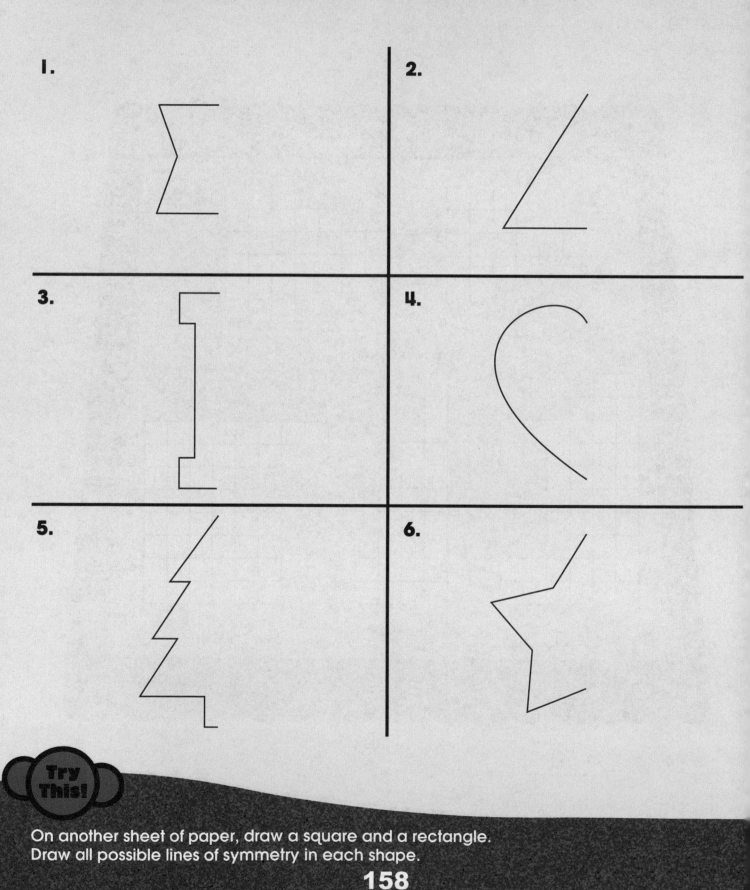

1.

2.

3.

4.

5.

6.

Try This!

On another sheet of paper, draw a square and a rectangle.
Draw all possible lines of symmetry in each shape.

Shape Up!

Directions: Complete the information for each polygon.

1.

Number of sides: _____

Name: _____

2.

Number of sides: _____

Name: _____

3.

Number of sides: _____

Name: _____

4.

Number of sides: _____

Name: _____

5.

Number of sides: _____

Name: _____

6.

Number of sides: _____

Name: _____

7.

Number of sides: _____

Name: _____

8.

Number of sides: _____

Name: _____

9.

Number of sides: _____

Name: _____

Try This!

Divide a sheet of paper in half. On one side, draw three polygons. On the other side, draw three non-polygons. Explain why they are not polygons.

Right, Acute, or Obtuse?

Directions: Write **right**, **acute**, or **obtuse** to describe each angle.

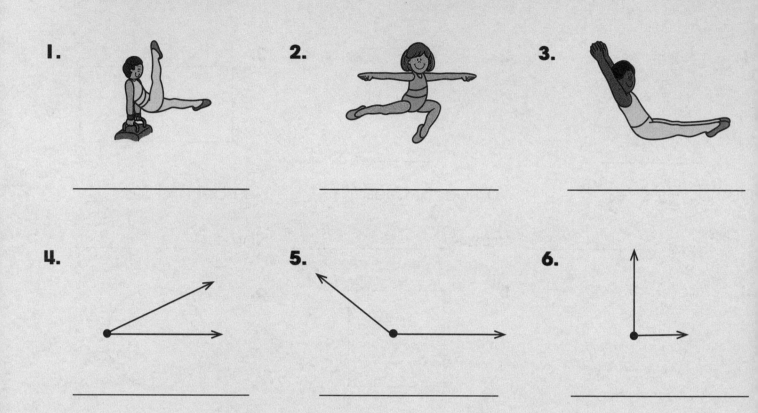

1. _____

2. _____

3. _____

4. _____

5. _____

6. _____

Directions: Trace the angle in each picture with a color.

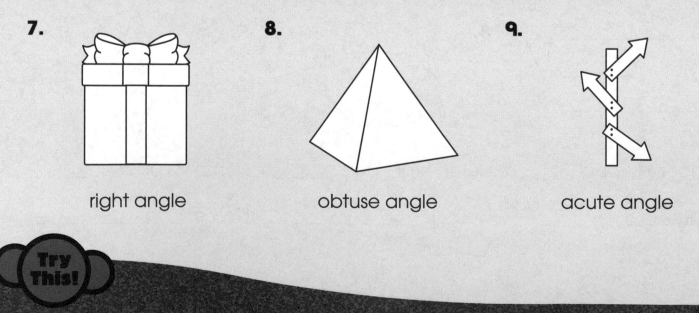

7. right angle

8. obtuse angle

9. acute angle

Try This!

Find examples of right, acute, and obtuse angles in your home.
List them on another sheet of paper.

Triangle Mysteries

Directions: Unscramble the letters to label each type of triangle.

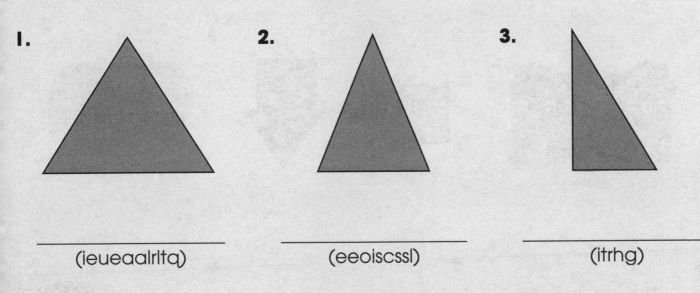

1.

2.

3.

_____   _____   _____
(ieueaalrlta)   (eeoiscssl)   (itrhg)

Directions: Draw a picture to match each description. Then, label each triangle.

4. Draw a triangle with one right angle.

5. Draw a triangle with all sides the same length.

6. Draw a triangle with only two sides the same length.

_____   _____   _____

On another sheet of paper, draw a picture of your favorite place to spend your free time. Use as many triangles as possible.

Flip, Slide, and Turn

Directions: Compare each pair of pictures. Tell how each picture changed by writing **flip**, **slide**, or **turn**.

1.

_____

2.

_____

3.

_____

4.

_____

5.

_____

6.

_____

7.

_____

8.

_____

9.

_____

Try This!

On another sheet of paper, draw a smiley face.
Then, draw it flipped, slid, and turned.

Solid Work

Directions: Write the name of each solid. Circle each vertex. Color each edge blue and each face yellow.

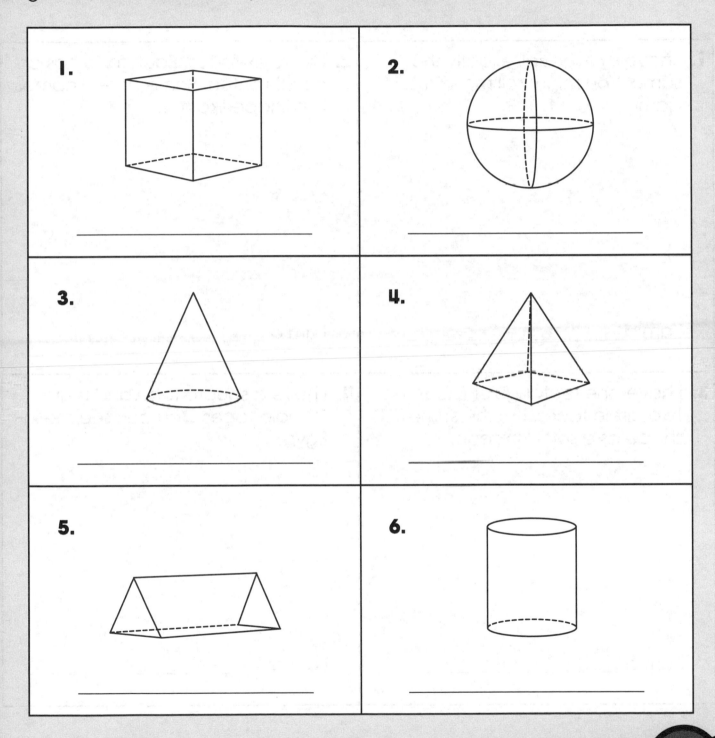

1. _____

2. _____

3. _____

4. _____

5. _____

6. _____

Try This!

Find examples of four geometric solids in your home. Draw them on another sheet of paper.

Directions: Read each riddle. Then, write the name of the solid described and draw a picture of it.

1. I have six faces all exactly the same. You might roll me in a game.

I am a _____.

2. I have six faces. Each face has an exact match. Some cereal comes in a shape like me.

I am a _____.

3. I have one rectangular face and two circle faces. I'm the same shape as a soft drink can.

I am a _____.

4. I have a square face and four triangle faces. You can see me in Egypt.

I am a _____.

Try This!

Write your own riddles for each solid.
Then, have a friend try to solve the riddles.

Picturing Pets Part 1

Directions: Noah collected data about his classmates' favorite pets. Color the graph to show the data he collected. Then, use the information on the graph to answer the questions on page 166.

Favorite Pets

cats	6
dogs	6
gerbils	4
goldfish	3
iguanas	1

Favorite Pets

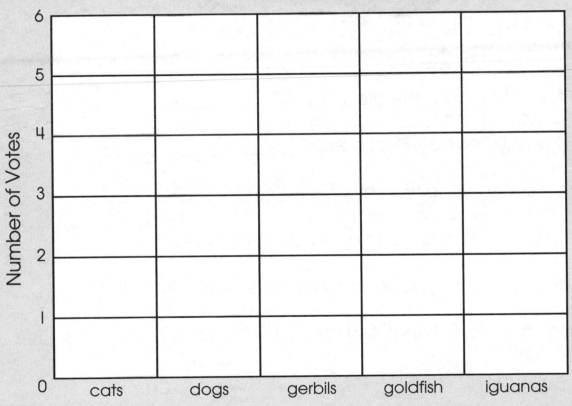

Number of Votes

cats   dogs   gerbils   goldfish   iguanas

Try This!

Collect data about your friends' and family members' favorite pets. Draw a graph to show the information.

Picturing Pets Part 2

Directions: Read the graph on page 165 and answer the questions.

1. What information does the graph show? _____

2. How many children voted for gerbils? _____

3. What pet received the fewest votes? _____

4. Which two pets received an equal number of votes? _____

5. How many votes did goldfish and gerbils receive altogether? _____

6. How many more children voted for cats than goldfish? _____

7. How many children voted in all? _____

8. What information does this graph *not* show? _____

Try This!

Draw pictures to add your own vote and the votes of three of your friends to the graph.

Hot Lunch Favorites

Directions: Banks asked 32 of his friends to name their favorite school lunches. He showed the information in a circle graph. Read the circle graph. Then, answer the questions.

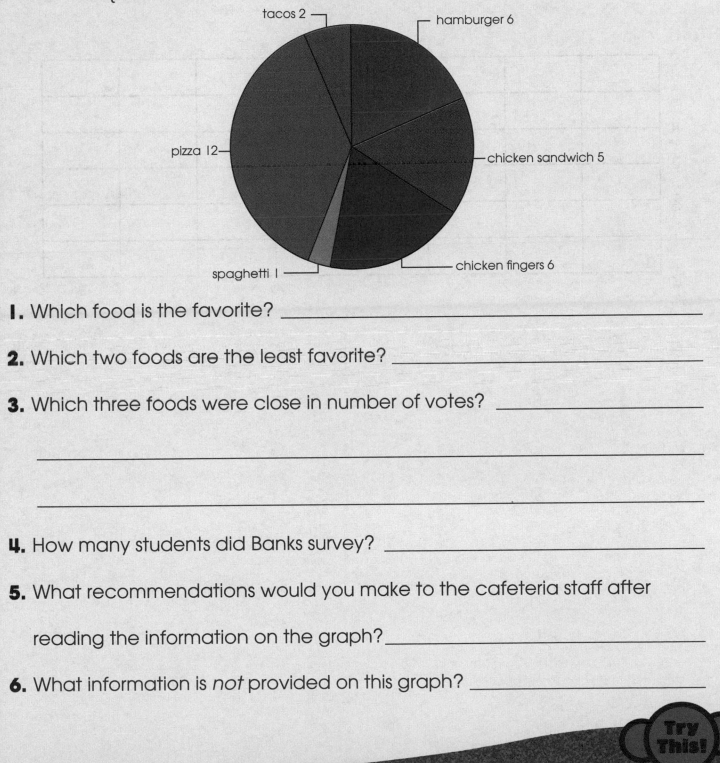

1. Which food is the favorite? _____

2. Which two foods are the least favorite? _____

3. Which three foods were close in number of votes? _____

_____

_____

4. How many students did Banks survey? _____

5. What recommendations would you make to the cafeteria staff after

reading the information on the graph? _____

6. What information is *not* provided on this graph? _____

Try This!

Write a letter to the cafeteria staff at Banks' school to tell them about the information Banks learned by taking the survey and creating a graph.

What a Pair!

Directions: Write the ordered pair for each letter. The first one has been done for you.

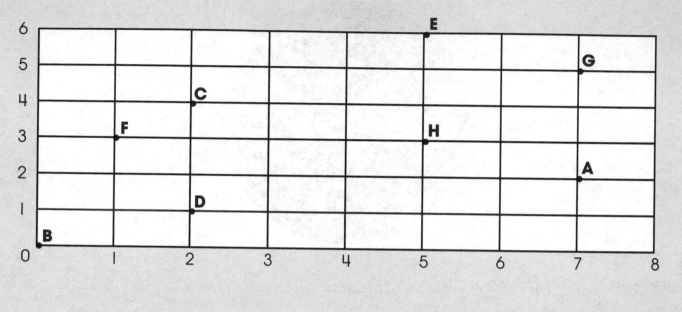

A ___(7,2)___   E _____

B _____   F _____

C _____   G _____

D _____   H _____

Try This!

On a sheet of grid paper, make a grid and place eight dots.
Then, write an ordered pair to describe each dot.

168

Delivery Time!

Directions: Write the letter of each ordered pair on the delivery map.

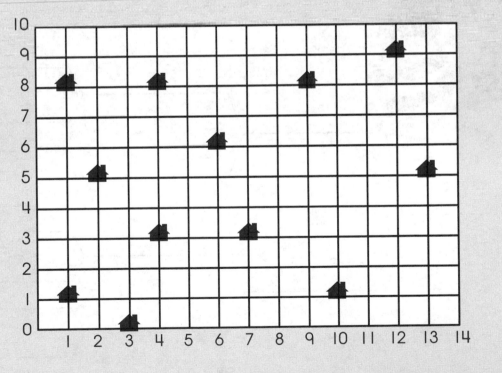

A. (3,0)   B. (4,3)   C. (7,3)   D. (6,6)   E. (9,8)   F. (12,9)

Use a red crayon to map out a different delivery route on the map above.
Mark each stop with an ordered pair.

Dress a Superhero

Directions: Complete the organizer to find all of the possible superhero costumes.

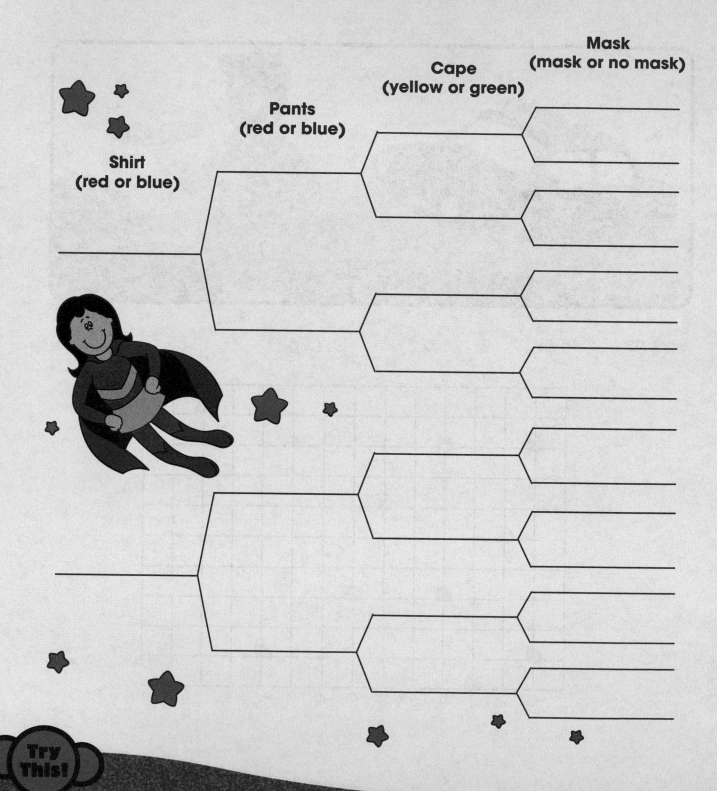

Shirt
(red or blue)

Pants
(red or blue)

Cape
(yellow or green)

Mask
(mask or no mask)

Try This!

On another sheet of paper, draw a picture of the superhero costume you would choose out of the options above.

What's Your Number?

Directions: Rearrange the numbers **4**, **6**, **8**, and **9** to find all of the possible four-digit numbers. Then, find the number that belongs to each student.

Possible Numbers

I. Lee has the largest number possible. What is Lee's number? _____

2. Shane has the smallest number possible. What is Shane's number? _____

3. Kaylen has the largest number with a 4 in the thousands place.

What is Kaylen's number? _____

4. Uri has the smallest number possible with the 9 in the tens place.

What is Uri's number? _____

Try This!

A palindrome is a word or a number that is the same whether it is written backward or forward. On another sheet of paper, list as many palindromes as you can.

What's in a Name?

Directions: Answer the questions using the tiles shown.

1. What is the probability of choosing an *M*? _____

2. What is the probability of choosing an *L*? _____

3. What is the probability of choosing a vowel? _____

4. What is the probability of choosing a consonant? _____

5. What is the probability of choosing an *A*? _____

6. What is the probability of choosing an *R*? _____

7. What is the probability of choosing a vowel? _____

8. What is the probability of choosing a consonant? _____

Try This!

Write the letters in your name on individual pieces of paper. Place the pieces in a hat and pull them out one at a time. Keep a tally of the letters you draw.

Fall in Line

Directions: Read each problem. Make a list of all of the possible solutions.

1. Lin, Shelby, and Quan are in line at the water fountain. In what different orders could they be standing?

2. Lin, Shelby, Quan, and Paul are in line. If Paul is always first, and Shelby is always second, how many different ways could the children line up?

3. Lin, Shelby, and Quan are in line in order from shortest to tallest. Shelby is taller than Lin. Quan is shorter than Shelby but taller than Lin. In what order are they standing?

4. Lin, Shelby, Quan, and Paul are in line. How many different ways can they line up if Lin is always first?

Try This!

On another sheet of paper, write your own word problem that requires making a list to solve it.

Funny Factory

Directions: Read each problem. Draw a picture to help you solve it.

1. The Funny Factory puts 5 pieces of trick gum in each pack. How many pieces of gum are in 4 packs?

2. The Funny Factory places 54 hand buzzers evenly into 9 boxes. How many buzzers are in each box?

3. Tyrone ordered 6 boxes of goofy glasses, but he returned 2 boxes. If 2 goofy glasses are in each box, how many goofy glasses did he keep?

4. Ansley wanted to buy some fake teeth. She had $10.00. Each package of fake teeth cost $0.75. How many packages of fake teeth could she buy?

Try This!

On another sheet of paper, write three more word problems about the Funny Factory. Draw a picture to show how to solve each problem.

Going on a Picnic

Directions: Use the tables to help you solve the problems.

1. Four ants—Anton, Greg, Fiona, and Brady—were carrying food back to the colony. They had an apple, a grape, a banana, and an orange. Anton did not carry anything round. Greg only likes red items. Brady does not like orange juice. What item did Anton, Greg, Fiona, and Brady each carry?

	apple	grape	banana	orange
Anton				
Greg				
Fiona				
Brady				

2. Kit, Liza, Luke, and Jimmy went on a picnic. They each brought a dish to share. Kit did not bring chicken or pizza. Jimmy loves pizza, but Luke does not like salad. Liza brought tamales. What dish did each person bring?

	salad	pizza	chicken	tamales
Kit				
Liza				
Luke				
Jimmy				

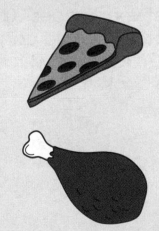

Try This!

On another sheet of paper, draw a picture of each person and ant at the picnic with his or her food.

Library Lessons

Directions: Read each problem. Use guess and check to help you solve it.

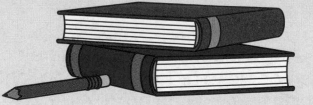

1. Jill opened a book. The pages she opened to were between 50 and 60. The sum of the two page numbers was 109. What pages did she open to?

2. Molly dropped a book on the floor. It opened to pages that were between 800 and 900. The sum of the two consecutive pages was 1,611. What pages did the book open to?

3. Taylor left his bookmark in his book. He left it somewhere between pages 200 and 300. The sum of the two page numbers is 597. Between which two pages is his bookmark?

4. Sam hid a dollar between two pages of his book. The two pages are between 900 and 1,000. The sum of the two page numbers is 1,829. Between which two pages did he hide the dollar?

Try This!

Open a book to any two pages. On another sheet of paper, write a problem about the two page numbers. Challenge a friend to solve your problem.

Super Skateboards

Directions: Read each problem. Look for a pattern to help you solve it.

1. Reese did 5 cool tricks on Monday, 7 cool tricks on Tuesday, and 9 cool tricks on Wednesday. How many tricks will he do on Saturday if this pattern continues?

Mon.	Tues.	Wed.	Thurs.	Fri.	Sat.
5	7	9			

What's the pattern? _____

2. Leigh designed a pattern for the top of her skateboard. She drew a triangle, a square, a triangle, and a square.

If this pattern continues, what will be the sixth shape she draws?

_____

3. At the skateboard tournament, the scores formed a pattern: 99, 90, 95, 86, and 91. If the pattern continues, what will be the eighth score?

1st	2nd	3rd	4th	5th	6th	7th	8th
99	90	95	86	91			

What is the pattern? _____

4. Brad fell off his skateboard 45 times the first day, 34 times the second day, and 23 times the third day. If this pattern continues, how many times will he fall on the fourth day?

1st	2nd	3rd	4th
45	34	23	

What is the pattern? _____

On another sheet of paper, draw your own pattern to put on a skateboard.

Shopping Spree

Directions: Read each problem. Work backward to help you solve it.

1. Tyrone got some money for his birthday. He spent $49.00 on a video game. He gave a friend $12.00. He also bought a new toy for $15.00. If he had $24.00 left over, how much did he start with?

2. Khalil walked from one side of the toy store to the other. It took him 5 minutes to walk from the video games to the race cars. Then, it took him 7 minutes to walk from the race cars to the board games. He got to the board games at 4:00 P.M. At what time did he leave the video games?

3. Right now, 20 toys are on the shelf. Five minutes ago, Kelly took 7 toys off of the shelf. Ten minutes ago, Luis took 3 toys off of the shelf. How many toys were on the shelf to begin with?

4. Noah spent $53.00 at the toy store. He bought a football for $10.00 and some trading cards for $20.00. He also bought some interlocking blocks. How much did he spend on the blocks?

Try This!

Imagine that you won a $100.00 shopping spree at your favorite store. Make a list on another sheet of paper of what you would buy.

Answer Key

Page 10
1. Baker; 2. Barnaby; 3. Casper; 4. Dylan: 5. Harmon; 6. Jersey; 7. Laramie; 8. Leghorn; 9. Lester; 10. Newton.

Page 11
bl words: blink, blow, (blip); *fl* words: fly, flip, (flow); *cl* words: clasp, climb, (clip), (clink).

Page 12
1. sw; 2. st; 3. tw; 4. st; 5. sw; 6. tw.

Page 13
1. scout; 2. mountain; 3. trout; 4. flower; 5. shout; 6. shower; 7. tower; 8. count.

Page 14
Row 1: thumb, shirt, cheese; Row 2: shoe, thorn, check; Row 3: chin, shell, thermos.

Page 15
1. tent; 2. nest; 3. raft; 4. ant; 5. plant; 6. forest; 7. soft; 8. footprint.

Page 16
Row 1: couch, brush, mouth; Row 2: wreath, bath, dish; Row 3: bench, fish, cloth.

Page 17
grasshopper; skateboard; grandmother; bookshelf; popcorn; doghouse.

Page 19
Answers will vary.

Page 20
1. are not; 2. she will; 3. you are; 4. he is; 5. you will; 6. we are; 7. they are; 8. I am; 9. cannot.

Page 21
remake; unopened; unknown; unkind; distrust; rewrap; disrespect.

Page 23
-er words: teacher, worker, driver; *-ful* words: beautiful, doubtful, thoughtful; *-less* words: colorless, careless, meaningless.

Page 25
Across: 1. government; 3. harden; 4. washable; 5. development; 9. shipment; Down: 2. readable; 6. lighten; 7. enjoyable; 8. tighten.

Page 26
Across: 2. section; 5. rhythm; 8. bandana; 9. rickety; Down: 1. academy; 3. lurch; 4. nation; 6. crate; 7. fancy.

Page 27
unlock and lock; strong and weak; cooked and raw; bad and good; present and absent; sharp and dull; small and big; buy and sell.

Page 28
1. a bare bear; 2. a hoarse horse; 3. a dear deer; 4. a knight night; 5. a weak week; 6. a fair fare; 7. feet feat; 8. aunt ant.

Page 29

1. yes; 2. yes; 3. no; 4. no; 5. yes; 6. no; 7. no; 8. yes.

Page 30

1. b. male deer; 2. b. alert or observant; 3. a. beat or pound; 4. a. fight; 5. a. hit; 6. b. look at closely.

Page 31

absorption (*n*); clay (*n*); compost (*n*); decompose (*v*); erosion (*n*); gravel (*n*); humidity (*n*); inorganic (*adj*); microbe (*n*); mineral (*n*); organic (*adj*).

Page 32

1. Look at the guide words. 2. noun, verb, and adjective; 3. two; 4. Answers will vary. 5. compost; 6. science; Answers will vary. 7. Answers will vary. 8. Answers will vary.

Page 33

Our class did an experiment with plants. (declarative) Wow, look at those plants grow! (exclamatory) Why isn't the plant growing in the dark? (interrogative) Water the plants every day. (imperative) What would happen if we fed the plants juice? (interrogative) It was so much fun doing a science experiment! (exclamatory) Record all data carefully. (imperative) Next time, we will see how plants grow with music. (declarative).

Page 35

1. NASA built a spacecraft called *Apollo 11*, and they launched it on July 16, 1969. 2. Four days later, *Apollo 11* reached the moon, and on July 20, Neil Armstrong and Buzz Aldrin walked on the moon. 3. The astronauts took many pictures of the moon, but they also collected 47 pounds of moon rocks. 4. You can read about their moonwalk online, or you can read about it in history books.

Page 36

1. work; 2. solve; 3. lose; 4. loses; 5. writes; 6. use; 7. keep; 8. know.

Page 37

present tense: twinkle, shoot, move, rise; past tense: sparkled, gazed, counted, looked; future tense: will shine, will watch, will fade, will name.

Page 38

Answers will vary.

Page 39

Answers will vary.

Page 40

Answers will vary.

Page 41

children; cities; sheep; knives; rashes; feet; cars; mice; ponies; halves; couches; dresses.

Page 42

Answers will vary.

Page 43
Answers will vary.

Page 44
Answers will vary.

Page 45
Answers will vary.

Page 46
1. Pilar created her own country. 2. She created her country on October 29, 2011. 3. What would her country be like? 4. What would be the law of the land? 5. She wanted all citizens to be equal. 6. Men, women, and children would have the same rights. 7. All races, religions, and cultures would be respected. 8. Everyone would live in peace.

Page 47
1. Juicy Frozen Fruit; 2. Sugar-Free Bubble Gum; 3. Instant Oatmeal; 4. Fruit Bar; 5. All-Natural Ice Cream; 6. Granola Bar.

Page 49
Topic sentence: The wind spreads seeds. Detail sentences: Dandelion seeds have parachutes. Maple seeds have wings. The wind picks up some seeds and carries them. Topic sentence: Animals spread seeds. Detail sentences: Some seeds with spikes attach to animals' fur. Some sticky seeds attach to the feet of some animals. Animals eat seeds and move them to other locations through their waste.

Page 51
Alexis and Emma's teacher gave them a research project. Alexis and Emma decided to research the history of money. First, they looked online for important information. Then, Alexis and Emma went to the local library. There, they checked out a book called The History of Money. Alexis read the book and then told Emma all about it. Emma wrote the information in a report. After the report was written, Alexis and Emma made a display. Finally, the girls presented their report to the class.

Page 53
6 Cook the pancakes until they are lightly browned on both sides.; 2 In a small bowl, mix together melted butter, egg, and milk.; 4 Have an adult help you spoon $\frac{1}{4}$ cup of the pancake batter on to a heated skillet.; 1 In a large bowl, mix together flour, sugar, baking powder, and salt. Set aside.; 5 When bubbles start to appear in the pancake, flip it over with a spatula.; 7 Serve the pancakes with your favorite pancake topping and enjoy.; 3 Add the egg mixture to the flour mixture. Stir until it is well blended.

Page 54
Answers will vary.

Page 55
Traveling in a space shuttle is fun. The astronauts can see Earth from a distance of 160 miles. Because the

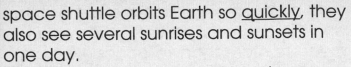

space shuttle orbits Earth so quickly, they also see several sunrises and sunsets in one day.

They pass over continents and oceans. It is very easy to see the United States and the Pacific Ocean from that distance.

The space shuttle travels around the whole world. It takes pictures and records data to bring back to NASA. The journey is incredible.

Page 56
Answers will vary.

Page 57
Answers will vary, but may include: 1. getting his picture taken; 2. unhappy; 3. photographer; 4. It was tight and uncomfortable.

Page 58
Setting: Los Angeles, CA, early morning, bedroom; Characters: Jeremy, Jeremy's mom; Theme: Jeremy has never been to the beach.

Page 59
Answers will vary.

Page 60
5 The alum and dirt sink to the bottom of the settling basin.; 3 From the reservoir, water goes into a mixing basin.; 7 The clean water is stored in a large storage tank.; 1 First raindrops fall into streams, lakes, and rivers.; 8 Water leaves the storage tank through water mains

and reaches your home through your faucets.; 4 Alum is added to take the dirt out of the water.; 6 Fluoride and chlorine are added to the water.; 2 Then, the streams and rivers flow into a reservoir.

Page 61
1. Daisy Lane, Tulip Avenue, Zinnia Road; 2. Zinnia Road and Sunflower Drive; 3. Tulip Avenue or Sunflower Drive; 4. Answers will vary but may include left on Daisy Lane, left on Daffodil Road, right on Zinnia Road, left on Violet Road, house is on left.

Page 62
Dog Tails: entertain; The Daily News: inform.

Page 63
Answers will vary but may include: 1. The baby birds, which were hungry and growing, were cared for by their mother. 2. Chirpy liked to jump near the edge of the nest. 3 Chirpy got too close to the edge one day and slipped, but his mother saved him.

Page 64
1. F; 2. O; 3. F; 4. F; 5. O; 6. F; 7. O; 8. F; 9. O; 10. O.

Page 65
1. Olivia; 2. Felipe; 3. Felipe; 4. Olivia; 5. Olivia; 6. Felipe; 7. Olivia; 8. Felipe.

Page 66
1. D; 2. A; 3. F; 4. E; 5. B; 6. G; 7. C; 8. H.

Page 67
1. cause; 2. effect; 3. effect; 4. cause; 5. effect; 6. cause; 7. cause; 8. effect; 9. effect; 10. cause.

Page 68
Millennium: green; Corkscrew: blue, yellow box, circled; Lightning: blue; Thunderbolt: red, circled; Anaconda: green, purple line; Copperhead: red, yellow box, circled; Avalanche: red, purple line, X; Mountain: blue; Thrill: nothing; Flashback: blue, purple line, circled; Speedy: blue; Hair-Raiser: red, purple line, circled; Splash: nothing; Twisted: blue; Backlash: blue, purple line, circled.

Page 69
Answers will vary.

Page 70
1. nonfiction; 2. to inform.

Page 71
1. fiction; 2. to entertain; 3. Frogs and Toads.

Page 72
1. Yellow: They are some of the best insect hunters. Bats help flowers and spread seeds. 2. Blue: More than 900 different kinds of bats; 3. Red: Although most bats eat only insects, some eat fruit and the nectar of flowers. 4. They can measure more than 16 inches (40.6 cm) long.

Page 73
Check that coloring and circling are correct. 1. Maria and Lucy; 2. the water park; 3. lazy river, wave pool, water slide, ate food; 4. last summer; 5. they won free tickets.

Page 74
Answers will vary.

Page 75
Skateboard for Sale
Black-and-white skateboard with royal blue wheels for sale. Like new. It was my favorite board ever. I need to sell it before I can buy in-line skates. Also comes with cool stickers. Cost is $8.00. Call 555-0123.
Bike for Sale
I am selling my favorite bike. I got it for my sixth birthday. The bike is blue with white stripes. Looks like new. I took really good care of it. Comes with a light and a basket. Cost is $15.00 or best offer. Call 555-0123.

Page 76
Answers will vary.

Page 77
Penguins: Life in Antarctica (nonfiction); Perry Penguin: Private Investigator (fiction); Shake, Rattle, and Roll: Famous

Earthquakes (nonfiction); Night of the Quakes (fiction); Moo! A Cow Joke Book (fiction); Moo! The Life of a Cow (nonfiction).

Page 79
1. historical fiction; 2. realistic fiction; 3. historical fiction; 4. realistic fiction.

Page 80
Answers will vary.

Page 81
Answers will vary.

Page 82
Answers will vary.

Page 83
Camping can be so much fun. **Last** weekend ~~me and~~ my family **and I** went camping in a park near the **mountains**. We took a lot of stuff because we weren't sure what we would need. Dad and I set up the tents, while Mom and my brother built a campfire and **made** lunch. After lunch, we went swimming in the lake. Later, we went fishing. **My** dad **caught** five fish! He cleaned **them** and cooked them over the campfire for **dinner**. They tasted **great**! After dinner, we **toasted** marshmallows and **told** scary **stories**. I wasn't really afraid. Finally, we crawled inside our tents to go to sleep. It was **quiet** except for the crickets. The next morning, we got up and **started** another day of fun. I love camping!

Page 84
Last year was **a lot** of fun. In **January**, we went skiing in **Denver**, Colorado. In **February**, my class performed a play about the life of **Martin** Luther **King, Jr**. I got to play the part of **Dr. King**. In the spring, my family spent a **week** at the **beach**. We **saw** two baby sharks **swimming** around the fishing pier! During the summer, I visited my **grandparents** in Texas. I visited the **Space Center** in **Houston**. Finally, in **December**, I had the best birthday ever! I got a puppy. I named him **Wolf** because he looks like a baby wolf. Last year was **really** a lot of fun. I hope next year will be even better!

Page 85
Answers will vary.

Page 86
Answers will vary.

Page 87
Answers will vary.

Page 89
Answers will vary.

Page 90
Answers will vary.

Page 91
Answers will vary.

Page 92
Answers will vary.

Page 93
Answers will vary.

Page 94
Answers will vary.

Page 96
1. 29; 2. 135; 3. 70; 4. 864; 5. 975; 6. 324; 7. 60; 8. 18.

Page 97
1. 9 tens, 1 ones; 2. 1 thousands, 9 hundreds, 8 tens, 9 ones; 3. 3 thousands, 5 hundreds, 1 tens, 4 ones; 4. 4 thousands, 3 hundreds, 2 tens, 1 ones; 5. 3 hundreds, 0 tens, 6 ones; 6. 1 thousands, 0 hundreds, 2 tens, 3 ones; 7. 1 thousands, 0 hundreds, 0 tens, 8 ones; 8. 9 thousands, 1 hundreds, 5 tens, 0 ones; 9. 6 thousands, 1 hundreds, 0 tens, 3 ones; 10. 2 thousands, 0 hundreds, 7 tens, 0 ones.

Page 98

¹3	5	0	²9		³8	7	⁴5	4
7	■		⁵1	⁶6	2		8	
⁷7	8	⁸2	■	7		⁹2	5	0
9	■	¹⁰5	1	3	¹¹2	4		
	¹²2				¹³9	6	0	¹⁴4
¹⁵7	0	0		¹⁶8	■	7	■	0
0				¹⁷6	6	4	8	0
1				1				0

Page 99
1. 936,700; 2. 200; 3. 64, 102; 4. 315,455; 5. 113,313; 6. 9,504; Labels: Zero in the Tens Place, One in the Ten Thousands Place.

Page 100
1. >; 2. =; 3. <; 4. <; 5. >; 6. =; 7. >; 8. >; 9. <; 10. <; 11. >; 12. >; 13. <; 14. <; Because they are smart "kids."

Page 101
938, 905, 869, 586, 570, 506, 403, 296, 234, 120.

Page 102
1. 5,732, 1,240, 932, 921; 2. 9,834, 5,685, 4,723, 960; 3. 4,323, 1,423, 1,238, 753; 4. 8,560, 4,086, 3,486, 235; 5. 3,483, 2,463, 301, 235; 6. 4,967, 3,023, 2,139, 587; 7. 4,672, 3,984, 2,164, 932; 8. 3,710, 1,236, 396, 256; 9. 9,325, 6,150, 4,356, 355; 10. 6,346, 2,356, 908, 823.

Page 103
1. 590; 2. 460; 3. 1,720; 4. 2,790; 5. 7,870; 6. 880; 7. 340; 8. 3,950; 9. 1,700; 10. 780; A "shampoodle"; 11. 900; 12. 800; 13. 700; 14. 3,200; 15. 1,900; 16. 6,100; 17. 4,800; A "bulldog."

Page 104
1. 82 orange; 2. 77 blue; 3. 51 yellow; 4. 35 red; 5. 96 green; 6. 52 red; 7. 73 orange; 8. 92 yellow; 9. 35 red; 10. 74 green.

Page 105

1. T: 810; 2. O: 813; 3. R: 733; 4. I: 747; 5. H: 675; 6. S: 631; 7. E: 976; 8. N: 919; 9. C: 802; 10. L: 815; Answer to riddle: THIRTEEN COLONIES.

Page 106

1. **12**; 2. 22; **3. 12**; 4. 32; **5. 12**; 6. 14; **7. 12**; **8. 12**.

Page 107

1. 112; 2. 110; 3. 100; 4. 102; 5. 119; 6. 114; 7. 116; 8. 105; 9. 101; 10. 104; 11. 107; 12. 113; 13. 120; 14. 103; 15. 109; 16. 238.

Page 108

1. **159**; 2. 185; 3. 142; 4. 289; **5. 159**; 6. 183; 7. 341; 8. 69; **9. 159**.

Page 109

Across: 1. 725; 3. 517; 4. 326; 6. 384; 8. 645; 10. 429; 12. 319; 14. 715; 16. 624; Down: 1. 747; 2. 583; 3. 543; 5. 206; 7. 459; 9. 489; 11. 255; 13. 176; 15. 108.

Page 110

1. B; 2. A; 3. B; 4. C; 5. D; 6. A.; 7. B; 8. C.

Page 111

1. 9; 2. 7; 3. 5; 4. 9, 9; 5. 3; 6. 9; 7. 7, 7; 8. 3, 3; 9. 3, 5.

Page 112

1. 2,425; 2. 2,148; 3. 5,246; 4. 3,289; 5. 5,408; 6. 8,209; 7. 2,182; 8. 6,249; 9. 6,428.

*	▲	#	♦	·	☺	□	▼	○
2	8	4	0	5	1	6	9	3

Page 113

1. a=5; 2. x=5; 3. s=18; 4. k=10; 5. n=8; 6. t=25; 7. a=39; 8. y=12; 9. x=425; 10. b=706.

Page 114

1. 76; 2. 9; 3. 104; 4. 24.

Page 115

1. D; 2. H; 3. B; 4. C; 5. F; 6. A; 7. E; 8. G.

Page 116

36	32	56		63	49		49	63	48	48	63	42	35		42	40	54	48
W	H	O		I	S		S	I	T	T	I	N	G		N	E	X	T

48	56		72	56	81
T	O		Y	O	U

Page 117

1. 1, 2, 3, 4, 5, 6, 7, 8, 9, 10, 11, 12; 2. 2, 4, 6, 8, 10, 12, 14, 16, 18, 20, 22, 24; 3. 3, 6, 9, 12, 15, 18, 21, 24, 27, 30, 33, 36; 4. 4, 8, 12, 16, 20, 24, 28, 32, 36, 40, 44, 48; 5. 5, 10, 15, 20, 25, 30, 35, 40, 45, 50, 55, 60; 6. 6, 12, 18, 24, 30, 36, 42, 48, 54, 60, 66, 72.

Page 119

7. 7, 14, 21, 28, 35, 42, 49, 56, 63, 70, 77, 84; 8. 8, 16, 24, 32, 40, 48, 56, 64, 72, 80, 88, 96; 9. 9, 18, 27, 36, 45, 54, 63, 72, 81, 90, 99, 108; 10. 10, 20, 30, 40, 50, 60, 70, 80, 90, 100, 110, 120; 11. 11, 22, 33, 44, 55, 66, 77, 88, 99, 110, 121, 132; 12. 12, 24, 36, 48, 60, 72, 84, 96, 108, 120, 132, 144.

Page 121

1. 3 horses with 4 legs each = 12 legs in all; 2. 5 spiders with 8 legs each = 40 legs in all; 3. 2 grasshoppers with 6 legs each = 12 legs in all; 4. 4 stools with 3 legs each = 12 legs in all; 5. 6 cows with 4 legs each = 24 legs in all; 6. 7 hens x 2 legs each = 14 in all.

Page 122

1. 184; 2. 86; 3. 69; 4. 80; 5. 99; 6. 124; 7. 84; 8. 147; 9. 99; 10. 48; 11. 155; 12. 186.

Page 123

1. 2; 2. 1; 3. 8; 4. 3; 5. 4; 6. 0; 7. 6; 8. 5; 9. 9; 10. 7.

Page 124

1. 312; 2. 224; 3. 38; 4. 132; 5. 135; 6. 34; 7. 275; 8. 152; 9. 58; 10. 657; 11. 161; 12. 192; 13. 372; 14. 656.

Page 125

1. F; 2. C; 3. G; 4. B; 5. E; 6. H; 7. A. 8. D.

Page 126

1. 3, 7; 2. 4, 9; 3. 7, 6; 4. 2, 7; 5. 10, 8; 6. 7, 3; 7. 3, 6; 8. 9, 5; 9. 11, 3; 10. 3, 5; 11. 3, 7; 12. 12, 8; 13. 7, 9; 14. 8, 5.

Page 127

12 ÷ 3 = 4, 12 ÷ 4 = 3, 3 x 4 = 12, 4 x 3 = 12; 24 ÷ 6 = 4, 24 ÷ 4 = 6, 6 x 4 = 24, 4 x 6 = 24; 28 ÷ 7 = 4, 28 ÷ 4 = 7, 7 x 4 = 28, 4 x 7 = 28; 36 ÷ 9 = 4, 36 ÷ 4 = 9, 9 x 4 = 36, 4 x 9 = 36; 40 ÷ 8 = 5, 40 ÷ 5 = 8, 8 x 5 = 40, 5 x 8 = 40; 63 ÷ 7 = 9, 63 ÷ 9 = 7, 7 x 9 = 63, 9 x 7 = 63; 35 ÷ 7 = 5, 35 ÷ 5 = 7, 7 x 5 = 35, 5 x 7 = 35; 54 ÷ 6 = 9, 54 ÷ 9 =6, 9 x 6 = 54, 6 x 9 = 54; 32 ÷ 8 = 4, 32 ÷ 4 = 8, 8 x 4 = 32, 4 x 8 = 32.

Page 128

1. 2 cookies; 2. 3 dog biscuits; 3. 5 pieces of pepperoni; 4. 6 books.

Page 129

1. 13; 2. 11; 3. 12; 4. 13; 5. 18; 6. 33; 7. 13; 8. 10; 9. 15; 10. 16; 11. 19; 12. 31; 13. 42; 14. 22; 15. 14; 16. 17.

Page 130

1. 9 r5; 2. 4 r2; 3. 16 r1; 4. 18 r1; 5. 13 r1; 6. 14 r2; 7. 16 r1; 8. 27 r1; 9. 12 r1; 10. 11 r5; 11. 16 r2; 12. 10 r4.

Page 131

E. 7 r2; T. 9 r1; D. 3 r3; S. 7 r4; I. 7 r3; B. 12 r1; U. 5 r3; H. 3 r2; A. 6 r2; N. 6 r1; R. 10 r7; G. 2 r2; Because their students are so bright!

Page 132

1. 4 bags; 2. 23 buckets; 3. 44 buckets; 4. 25 cups; 5. Ana; 6. 19 cups. Cody popped fewer than Ana.

Page 133

1. x; 2. ÷; 3. –; 4. +; 5. –; 6. +; 7. –; 8. x; 9. –; 10. ÷; 11. ÷; 12. x; 13. ÷; 14. –.

Page 134

1. 42¢; 2. 66¢; 3. 97¢; 4. 73¢; 5. 88¢; 6. 80¢.

Answer Key

Page 135

	Amount	Quarters	Dimes	Nickels	Pennies
1.	$0.76	3	0	0	1
2.	$0.45	1	2	0	0
3.	$0.98	3	2	0	3
4.	$0.40	1	1	1	0
5.	$0.84	3	0	1	4
6.	$0.62	2	1	0	2
7.	$1.42	5	1	1	2
8.	$1.68	6	1	1	3

Page 136
1. $50.42; 2. $43.94; 3. $44.13; 4. $22.79; 5. $51.00; 6. $80.73; 7. $44.45; 8. $65.76; 9. $65.70.

Page 137
1. $19.50; 2. $2.39; 3. $9.16; 4. $12.97; 5. $14.20; 6. $7.49.

Page 138
Answers will vary.

Page 139
1. $5.45; 2. $5.00; 3. $10.00; 4. $7.75.

Page 140
puzzle, $2.00; football, $9.00; wind-up car, $20.00; board game, $6.00; baseball, $4.00; blocks, $4.00; video game, $19.00; teddy bear, $17.00; doll, $12.00.

Page 141

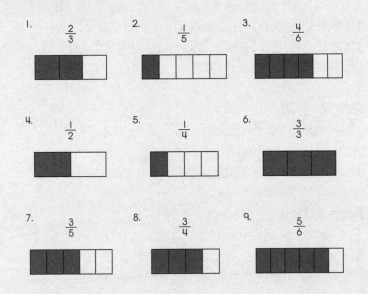

1. $\frac{2}{3}$ 2. $\frac{1}{5}$ 3. $\frac{4}{6}$

4. $\frac{1}{2}$ 5. $\frac{1}{4}$ 6. $\frac{3}{3}$

7. $\frac{3}{5}$ 8. $\frac{3}{4}$ 9. $\frac{5}{6}$

Page 142
1. C; 2. A; 3. D; 4. B; 5. E.

Page 143
$$\frac{1}{2} = \frac{2}{4}, \frac{4}{8}, \frac{3}{6}; \frac{1}{3} = \frac{2}{6}, \frac{3}{9}, \frac{4}{12}, \frac{1}{4}$$
$$= \frac{2}{8}, \frac{4}{16}, \frac{3}{12}.$$

Page 145
1. $\frac{2}{3} > \frac{1}{3}$; 2. $\frac{1}{4} = \frac{2}{8}$; 3. $\frac{3}{8} < \frac{2}{3}$; 4. $\frac{3}{7} > \frac{3}{8}$; 5. $\frac{3}{4} < \frac{4}{5}$; 6. $\frac{3}{6} = \frac{6}{12}$.

Page 146
1. 3 inches, 8 cm; 2. 3 inches, 7 cm; 3. 4 $\frac{1}{2}$ inches, 11 cm; 4. 4 inches, 10 cm; 5. 1 inch, 3 cm; 6. 3 $\frac{1}{2}$ inches, 9 cm.

Page 147
1. 36 feet; 2. 60 inches; 3. 2 feet; 4. 72 inches; 5. 216 inches; 6. 4 yards; 7. 48 inches; 8. 63 feet; 9. 3 feet 3 inches; 10. 45 feet or 540 inches.

Page 148
1. 4 cups; 2. 8 quarts; 3. 16 cups; 4. 32 pints; 5. 6 cups; 6. 12 cups; 7. 2 gallons; 8. 16 quarts; 9. 2 gallons; 10. 8 pints.

Page 149
1. ounces; 2. pounds; 3. pounds; 4. tons; 5. pounds; 6. ounces; 7. tons; 8. tons; 9. ounces.

Page 150
1. B; 2. H; 3. A. 4. G; 5. C; 6. F; 7. D; 8. E.

Page 151
1. 60 inches; 2. 4; 3. 5 ft.; 4. yes.

Page 152
80°F; 50°C; 30°C; 90°F.

Page 153
1. 7:00; 2. 1:30; 3. 2:00; 4. 11:00; 5. 4:30; 6. 12:30; 7. 3:15; 8. 2:45; 9. 9:15.

Page 154
1. 7:00 A.M.; 2. 12:30 P.M.; 3. 2:00 P.M.; 4. 10:20 P.M.; 5. 8:57 P.M.; 6. 8 hours.

Page 155
1. 6:30, 8:00, 1 hour, 30 minutes; 2. 7:00, 8:45, 1 hour, 45 minutes; 3. 9:10, 5:10, 8 hours; 4. 1:30, 8:15, 6 hours, 45 minutes; 5. 11:00, 3:45, 4 hours, 45 minutes; 6. 2:30, 6:45, 4 hours, 15 minutes.

Page 156
1. 10 square units; 2. 6 square units; 3. 6 square units; 4. 9 square units; 5. 4 square units; 6. 6 square units.

Page 157
1. 24 units; 2. 26 units; 3. 36 units; 4. 28 units; 5. 36 units.

Page 158
Answers will vary but should show an understanding of symmetry.

Page 159
1. 3, triangle; 2. 6, hexagon; 3. 4, rectangle; 4. 5, pentagon; 5. 4, square; 6. 0, circle; 7. 4, parallelogram; 8. 8, octagon; 9. 4, rhombus.

Page 160
1. right angle; 2. acute angle; 3. obtuse angle; 4. acute angle; 5. obtuse angle; 6. right angle;

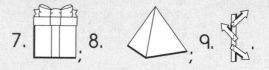
7. ; 8. ; 9.

Page 161
1. equilateral; 2. isosceles; 3. right; 4. right; 5. equilateral; 6. isosceles.

Page 162
1. flip; 2. turn; 3. slide; 4. flip; 5. turn; 6. slide; 7. turn; 8. flip; 9. slide.

Page 163

1. cube; 2. sphere; 3. cone; 4. square pyramid; 5. rectangular prism; 6. cylinder.

Page 164

1. cube; 2. rectangular prism; 3. cylinder; 4. square pyramid.

Page 165

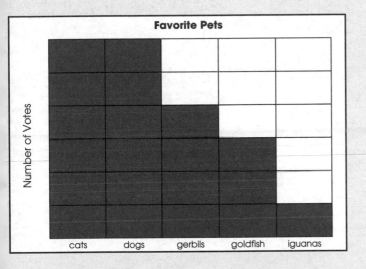

Page 166

1. Noah's classmates' favorite pets; 2. 4; 3. iguana; 4. dogs and cats; 5. 7; 6. 3; 7. 20; 8. Answers will vary.

Page 167

1. pizza; 2. tacos and spaghetti; 3. hamburgers, chicken sandwich, and chicken fingers; 4. 32; 5. Answers will vary. 6. Answers will vary.

Page 168

A. (7,2); B. (0,0); C. (2,4); D. (2,1); E. (5,6); F. (1,3); G. (7,5); H. (5,3).

Page 169

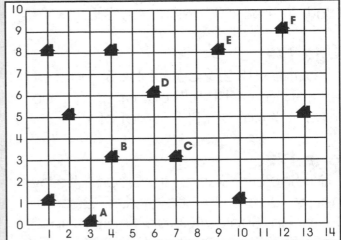

Page 170

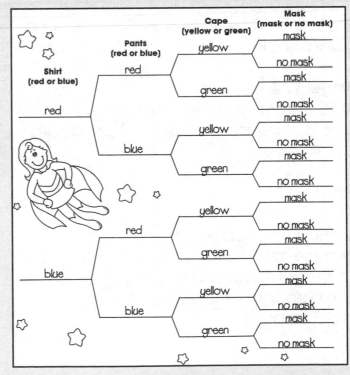

Page 171

4,689; 4,698; 4,869; 4,896; 4,986; 4,968;

6,489; 6,498; 6,894; 6,849; 6,948; 6,984; 8,469; 8,496; 8,964; 8,946; 8,649; 8,694; 9,846; 9,864; 9,684; 9,648; 9,486; 9,468; 1. 9,864; 2. 4,689; 3. 4,986; 4. 4,698.

Page 172
1. 1 out of 14; 2. 2 out of 14; 3. 5 out of 14; 4. 9 out of 14; 5. 4 out of 13; 6. 2 out of 13; 7. 7 out of 13; 8. 6 out of 13.

Page 173
1. Lin, Shelby, Quan; Lin, Quan, Shelby; Shelby, Quan, Lin; Shelby, Lin, Quan; Quan, Lin, Shelby; Quan, Shelby, Lin; 2. two ways (Paul, Shelby, Lin, Quan; Paul, Shelby, Quan, Lin); 3. Lin, Quan, Shelby; 4. six ways (Lin, Shelby, Quan, Paul; Lin, Shelby, Paul, Quan; Lin, Quan, Paul, Shelby; Lin, Quan, Shelby, Paul; Lin, Paul, Quan, Shelby; Lin, Paul, Shelby, Quan).

Page 174
1. 20 pieces of gum; 2. 6 buzzers in each box; 3. 8 goofy glasses; 4. 13 packages of fake teeth.

Page 175
1. Anton carried the banana, Greg carried the apple, Fiona carried the orange, and Brady carried the grape. 2. Kit brought salad, Liza brought tamales, Luke brought chicken, and Jimmy brought pizza.

Page 176
1. pages 54 and 55; 2. pages 805 and 806; 3. pages 298 and 299; 4. pages 914 and 915.

Page 177
1. 15 tricks, the pattern is +2; 2. a square; 3. 78, the pattern is –9, +5; 4. 12 times, the pattern is –11.

Page 178
1. $100.00; 2. 3:48 P.M.; 3. 30 toys; 4. $23.00.